ODILON REDON | GUSTAVE MOREAU | RODOLPHE BRESDIN

The Museum of Modern Art, New York

in collaboration with The Art Institute of Chicago

Distributed by Doubleday & Co., Inc., Garden City, New York

EXHIBITION DATES

The Museum of Modern Art, New York:
  December 4, 1961 – February 4, 1962

The Art Institute of Chicago:
  March 2, 1962 – April 15, 1962

Library of Congress Catalogue Card
  Number 61-17804

The Museum of Modern Art, 1961
  11 West 53 Street, New York 19, N.Y.

Printed in Germany by Brüder Hartmann,
  West Berlin

CONTENTS

Nothing is more pleasant than to render justice where it is due. To impart homage to three artists simultaneously provides a threefold satisfaction, for among them only one is famous, whereas the name of the second is better known than his work, and the third has all but escaped attention. Moreover, Redon's considerable renown is based mostly on his exquisite flowerpieces, whereas his frequently more significant paintings, pastels, drawings, and lithographs of imaginary subjects do not yet enjoy the favor they deserve. It is in these works, on which particular stress has been put in the present exhibition, that he explored a world of dreams which his contemporary, Moreau—fifteen years his elder—also penetrated, though from a completely different angle. Yet if Moreau had painted only the jewel-laden compositions for which he was admired during his lifetime, he probably would have occupied merely a niche reserved for illustrators in the history of art. But he has done more: not only was he the teacher of Matisse and Rouault, a circumstance which has kept his name alive while his own work remained in shadow, he even ventured with considerable boldness into a type of "abstraction" far more radical than anything that was being done in his day. These endeavors are little known and have never before been exhibited in this country. As in the case of Redon, a special effort has therefore been made to show Moreau in the light of his least known and perhaps most remarkable contributions.

Bresdin, a man of lesser stature though by no means an artist to be neglected, was the master of Redon who warmly admired him; yet this did not save him from oblivion. But it would have been a grievous mistake to omit him from this exhibition devoted to works that can be considered forerunners of surrealism and that represent a frequently overlooked current of the last century, buried beneath the more powerful trends of realism and impressionism. Beyond his personal link with Redon, Bresdin has much to offer that will be of value to those who search for the expression of fantasy in art.

In preparing this exhibition, it has been a gratifying surprise to discover that a great many of Redon's important works are now publicly or privately owned in this country. This wealth has been supplemented by a few loans from abroad to achieve a well-rounded representation of the artist's evolution. But because of their fragility only locally owned pastels have been included, save a few which can safely travel. In gathering the section devoted to Redon, I had the good fortune to receive the most complete assistance and counsel from my friend Arï Redon in Paris, the master's only son, who devotes himself with discreet but deep fervor to the memory of his father. Not only did he allow me to draw on his own collection whenever called for, he has also been particularly helpful in the arduous task of dating Redon's works, consulting, as far as possible, his father's private notes.

It would have been impossible to represent Moreau properly without the generous support of the French authorities who made available the treasures of the Musée Gustave Moreau in Paris. Indeed, the artist—reluctant to part with his works—left his entire collection to the state, to be kept as a museum in the very house and studio which he occupied during his entire life. But since these premises are scarcely appropriate for the display of paintings, they attract too few visitors. It is even said that the gloomy atmosphere of the place dissuaded Degas, once a friend of Moreau, from making a similar bequest. The Musée Gustave Moreau is particularly rich in those small canvases in which the artist so completely abandoned the minute details of his large compositions (most of them too fragile to be borrowed) and achieved an astonishing freedom of expression. That these intriguing works, which have never left France before, could be so well represented in this exhibition is due to the understanding and gracious cooperation of M. Henri Seyrig, Director General of French Museums, assisted in this instance by Mme de la Roche-Vernet Henraux, to whom I am also deeply indebted.

The section devoted to Moreau was assembled by Miss Dore Ashton, who wishes to acknowledge gratefully the advice she received from M. Julien Alvard, M. Jean Paladilhe, Curator of the Musée Gustave Moreau, Mr. Robert Pincus-Witten, Mlle Isabelle Rouault, and M. Georges Salles, as well as from Mr. Peter Selz. Wherever possible, works by Moreau have been borrowed from American collections. However, the only major group owned in this country was left to the Fogg Art Museum in Cambridge under restrictions imposed by the donor which prevent its being lent.

The gathering of significant works by Bresdin presented little difficulty, the late Walter S. Brewster having given an extensive collection of prints and drawings to the Art Institute of Chicago. The sections devoted to Bresdin and to the graphic work of Redon were selected by Mr. Harold Joachim, Curator of Prints and Drawings of the Art Institute.

My thanks are due to those who in many ways helped make this exhibition possible, to the numerous lenders, listed on page 172, and to those whose generosity aided in the production of this book; to Messrs. Hirschl and Adler, and to Mr. Eugene Victor Thaw, of New York for valuable advice, to M. Pierre Boulat for use of his color transparencies (pages 109, 127, 135 and 143), and to Mr. Hyman Swetzoff of Boston for assistance with the translation of Redon's writings on Bresdin. Miss Constance Clodfelter was most helpful in assembling the catalogue.

JOHN REWALD, *Director of the Exhibition*

for Arï Redon

Redon was born in Bordeaux on April 20, 1840, shortly after his parents arrived from America. His father had gone to Louisiana to replenish the family fortune, lost during the Napoleonic Wars, and there married a four-teen-year-old French girl, native of New Orleans, who in 1835 bore him a first son, Ernest. The mother once told her second son, Odilon, that she had seen a sea-monster during the trip back to France. He himself later said he should have preferred that the ship which carried his parents be delayed during the voyage so that he might have seen the day on the high seas. This wish, had it been fulfilled, would have enhanced with a single eccentric note a biography otherwise utterly devoid of the spectacular or picturesque.

Indeed, the life of Redon, whose visions were so tenaciously concerned with the extraordinary, whose imagination constantly dwelled on the confines of the supernatural, was absolutely quiet and discreet, a per-fect image of the man himself. It was the exact opposite of the celebrated *vie de bohême* which Murger so elo-quently described in the days when Redon was raised on an isolated estate near Bordeaux. As the silent and sickly child grew into a gentle and shy adolescent he, who had no fear of horror, instinctively abhorred all that was ostentatious, disorderly, vulgar. The loud and obvious manifestations of youth, the uncouthness and stupidity of provincialism inspired him with such aver-sion that the life upon which he embarked was to be guided by an overpowering desire for seclusion, con-templation, and creativity.

Partly on account of his frail health and partly because of a certain indifference of his parents, Odilon Redon was sent at a very tender age to live with an old uncle at Peyrelebade, a property of the family which his father had been able to repurchase with gains real-ized in America. This large domain in the midst of marshes and vineyards lay in a shallow region once covered by the ocean. Its big, sixteenth-century house, surrounded by an abandoned park with unruly vege-tation, became the ideal haunt for the youngster who liked to isolate himself, to dream, to read, to listen to music, and to hear tales of sorcerers from the peasants who still believed in them. His brother Ernest was a musical prodigy. "When I was born," Redon once said, "he already played; still in the cradle, I heard Beethoven and Bach. I was born on a sound wave. There is not a recollection of my early childhood which is not linked to a melody, to music of quality. Later, as an adolescent, I listened to then still little-known works by Berlioz, Schumann, Chopin. Our family home was filled with it. Music certainly left its mark on my soul."[1]

Stretched out under some gnarled tree, the child watched clouds sweep over the flat lands, interpreted their ever changing patterns, followed their moving shapes towards the distant horizon. The weird beings they suggested to him became his favorite companions. Although he did not say so expressly when he later fondly remembered those days, it would seem, from the images he was subsequently to create so abundantly, that the things which clouds and nature evoked in him were fraught with terrors. Yet the very fact that he felt himself surrounded by strange and fearful mon-sters caused him to lose all apprehension of them, so that he could treat them with the same innocent famili-arity with which other children consort with fairies, elves, or angels.

The young Redon was particularly fascinated by the intricate forms of branches, outlined like specters against the sky. He never relinquished a deep love for trees and relished the sad sound of pines shaken by the wind. Among birds he favored owls. He preferred soft shadows to glaring light, steeped himself in poetry, drew, meditated, played the violin, and almost feverishly absorbed the spectacles of nature which the arid and yet savage landscape round Peyrelebade provided. Even the human beings, the peasants and laborers whom he observed, added a freakish note to the atmosphere of his childhood. One of his acquaintances later reported that the faces met in this area "translate almost

Redon: *Head of an Old Woman*. (1875–80). Charcoal, 14³/₈ × 11⁵/₈″. Rijksmuseum Kröller-Müller, Otterlo

invariably a certain weariness of life. Some show the signs of resignation, others the indelible marks of vice or idiocy. The heredity of these stagnant populations is so heavy that no expression of joy is possible. Eventually this was to make him gloomy, as if he himself felt flowing in his veins the blood of those slow, morose, almost fossil beings he knew as a child. And as a natural consequence the receding brows and protuberances of those heads, and the asymmetry of those features were to engrave themselves in his mind. Finally, he was to remember, to the extent of being obsessed by it, the steady gaze, burning or dull, of eyes rotating in enormous sockets."[2]

In the peace of his early life, troubled by impressions rather than by happenings, and dominated by an awesome imagination, there grew in Redon a profound attraction for violence, movement, even terror. When at the age of seven he spent a year in Paris and for the first time was taken to a museum, only the most romantic and dramatic paintings struck his fancy and lingered in his memory. His boundless admiration for Delacroix was the direct result of this initial encounter with art; his preference for Beethoven followed a similar inclination.

Nearly all of Redon's interests, his predilections and tendencies can be traced to childhood recollections and adventures. Nothing that he ever experienced seems to have been lost. Every observation and emotion joined the rich store of impressions on which he was to draw for many years to come. With an almost unbelievable lucidity he absorbed whatever came his way: the texture of decrepit masonry, the arabesque of a leaf, the fleeting and often disquieting forms of clouds, the depressive traits of a farmer, even familiar or unfamiliar sounds. And he freely mixed what he saw with what he imagined, refusing to distinguish between these two experiences. At the same time a strange kind of logic seems to have reigned over the mind of the lonesome youngster who more or less consciously accumulated an

10

incredible wealth of sensations. Saturated though he was with all that silent hours had taught him, there was not the slightest disorder among the multitude of perceptions.

Thus, from his earliest days on, anything that struck his eager curiosity seems to have been destined to serve the artist who grew up in Redon. This almost involuntary singlemindedness—for these pictorial or sensorial recollections began to amass before he actually became aware of his calling—was to remain characteristic of the mature man who throughout his life never deviated from the road which destiny appeared to have traced for him. Looking back, he was to say many years later: "I believe I have given in docilely to the secret laws which prompted me to create—as best I could, and according to my dreams—things into which I put all of myself."[3]

That Redon's work drew much of its strength from ineffaceable childhood impressions is not merely a supposition based on the peculiar *House of Usher* atmosphere in which he grew up, virtually abandoned to himself, or on the fact that he was a frail child whose imagination was ever active. It is a circumstance on which he has insisted again and again in an effort to explain to others and to himself the strange visions visited upon him. More than half a century later he stated: "I owe to my country those sorrowful faces…which I have drawn because I have seen them and because my eyes, as a child, had preserved them for the intimate echoes of my soul. Yes, an ancient wall, an old tree, a certain horizon can be nourishment and a vital element for an artist—there, where he has his roots."[4] And after he revisited Peyrelebade shortly before his death, he told a friend: "I have completely understood the origins of the sad art I have created. It is a site for a monastery, an enclosure in which one feels oneself alone—what abandon! It was necessary there to fill one's imagination with the unlikely, for into this exile one had to put something. After all, it may well be that in places most completely deprived of features pleasant to the eye the spirit and the imagination must take their revenge."[5]

Despite the purposefulness, not to say the inevitability, with which the child prepared countless treasures for the invention of the man, Redon's evolution was by no means a simple or painless one. He was not spared the doubts and sufferings experienced by those who feel the urge to create and at the same time fear their gifts to be insufficient. For a while he was not even sure in which medium these gifts were to find their expression. Only one thing appeared to be certain: that the early impressions, the untold dreams, the vague aspirations had to be cast into some artistic form. But the very nature of his creative sources and impulses forcibly set him apart from the various positivist currents of his time, thus for a long time preventing others from appreciating his original talent, from sharing the world of his turbulent fancy. The lonely child was to become a lonely man, seemingly destined for unending isolation.

At the age of eleven Redon was finally sent to classes in Bordeaux. After the years of idyllic solitude at Peyrelebade the adjustment proved difficult. His school years were unpleasant, a chain of sufferings which translated themselves into rather mediocre marks. His first communion, however, was to stir him deeply, not because of devout prayers but because his mystical fervor could feast on liturgical music and stained-glass windows. Henceforth he visited churches and chapels to listen to the choir. His only interests were music and drawing. At the beginning these tastes were encouraged by his family which permitted him, when he was fifteen, to take drawing lessons with a local artist, Stanislas Gorin. The boy who had received so little affection from his mother found in Gorin a man who understood his secret longings and appreciated his natural gifts. His teacher incited him to observe more consciously, to make copies, to study the works of such masters as Delacroix, but above all he taught him never to draw a line except under the dictate of both his sensitivity and his reason, warning him against the dangerous temptations of routine. Redon owed a tremendous debt to his unusually liberal mentor. Instead of warping his emerging personality, Gorin strenghtened it and guided it toward the highest goals. Although he insisted that his pupil study nature objectively, Redon soon preferred, as he later said, "to attempt the representation of imaginary things which haunted me, representation in which I failed at the beginning. Just the same I did many landscapes, battle scenes, evocations of scattered figures in rocky plains, an entire world of despair, filled with the black fumes of romanticism that still surrounded me."[3] There can be little doubt that these early, melancholy images reflected many of the dreams with which the child had animated his solitude at Peyrelebade.

Simultaneously, the young Redon visited local exhibitions to which many Parisian artists sent their paintings and where he acquainted himself not only with the works of the revered Delacroix, but also with those of Millet, Corot, and Gustave Moreau, then still a beginner. He discussed his observations with his master who kindled his ardor and helped him establish his enthusiasms on the firm ground of understanding and knowledge. Above all, Gorin shared his student's fervor for Delacroix to whom Redon later attributed "the first awakening and the sustenance of my own flame."[6]

Gorin also spoke to his pupil of literature and music. Yet it was an encounter with the botanist Armand Clavaud, whom he met a little later and who was a few years older than he, which opened to him new horizons on the literary arts. Clavaud acquainted his young friend not only with Hindu poetry and the philosophy of Spinoza, but also with contemporary writing, lending him recently published books by controversial authors such as Flaubert, Poe, and Baudelaire. How could the juvenile painter fail to appreciate the subtle psychology of Flaubert, cast in a supremely elegant style; how could he not discover in Poe's texts, translated by Bau-

delaire, innumerable somber images akin to his own dreams; and above all, how could he resist the ardent rhythms, the melodious verses of Baudelaire, poetic equivalent of Delacroix's paintings? In Baudelaire's poems Redon found expressed a peculiar "spleen," a predilection for the macabre which struck a chord in his own soul.[7]

The true initiation which distasteful school years had been unable to provide, Redon derived from the pages of Flaubert, Poe, and Baudelaire. But Clavaud also interested him in his own work, specialized, as Redon was to put it, "in the confines of the imperceptible, that intermediate state between animal and plant life, of flower or being, that mysterious element which is animal for a few hours of the day but only under the action of light."[3] He who had always been fascinated by all that was mysterious now was permitted to approach a new kind of mystery, hidden in the very depth of nature itself.

It seems quite extraordinary that a young man born in the provinces, raised on an isolated estate with few outside contacts, should have been able to study the works of modern masters, to hear good music, to read new and significant books, in a word to enter life under such favorable auspices. But when, around 1857, he left school and wished to become a painter, his father insisted that he study architecture instead. Redon obeyed, although he continued to draw and to paint, even participating in local exhibitions, while working with various architects in Bordeaux. Whereas his architectural apprenticeship failed to arouse his enthusiasm, Redon did not consider it a waste.

"Nothing is lost in studying," he was to write later. "I believe that I owe much, as a painter, to what I learned as an aspiring architect: for instance, the projection of shadows which an enlightened professor made me draw with meticulous attention, basing abstract theories on demonstrations with tangible bodies; and suggesting, for the problems to be solved, special cases of shadows projected on spheres or other solid forms. This was to serve me later; I more easily approached the unlikely by means of the likely and could give visual logic to the imaginary elements which I perceived."[3]

During one of his short visits to Paris which helped him escape the stifling atmosphere of Bordeaux and the boredom of his architectural studies, Redon saw Delacroix—from afar. This happened in 1859. Redon never tired of recalling that Delacroix had appeared to him "as beautiful as a tiger; the same pride, the same litheness, the same strength. It was at an official ball given at the Préfecture and I had been told that he would be there. My brother Ernest who accompanied me didn't know him anymore than I did, yet instinctively he pointed out to me a small, aristrocratic figure, standing by himself in the ballroom, in front of a group of seated women. Long black hair, drooping shoulders, stooped pose. We approached him discreetly and the master, for it was he, raised toward us that unique, blinking gaze which darted with more brightness than the chandeliers. A personage of the utmost distinction. . . .

"He was of medium height, thin, and nervous. We watched him during all that evening in the midst of the crowd and even left at the same time he did, behind him. We followed him. He passed through the nocturnal Paris alone, head bent, walking like a cat. . . ."[6] The many impressions which already peopled the imagination of Redon thus were joined by the shadow of a venerated man, a lonely figure in the stillness of sleeping Paris.

Yet not all his visits to the capital left such recollections. On the advice of Gorin, whom he continued to see and consult frequently, Redon, two years later, at the age of twenty-one, returned there for three months but complained that they were nightmarish. Back home he found relief in a short trip to the Pyrenees which he undertook with a friend. That pictorial expression continued to be his main preoccupation must have appeared clearly in his letters home, since his brother, in a reply, voiced the hope that this excursion would be a great benefit to him, "for this is altogether your type of landscape: mountains, dismal solitudes, despair. How you are going to brush, scrape, rub, devour your canvas after your return! All those beautiful sites will haunt you and you will brood over them in order to translate them. Then, one fine morning, you will deliver yourself of some fantastic, antediluvian landscape, one of those somber and desolate scenes. . . ."[8]

Indeed, more than thirty years later, Redon still remembered vividly the durable and profound impressions of this trip, "the rocks scorched by the sun, the sad sands, the desolate solitudes."[1] He kept in his "retina the fanatical and burning brilliance of certain gazes perceived in poor villages, admirably consumed by distress. Round Pamplona, on the plateau of the Spanish Biscaya, what I saw was one of the most decisive sensations I have experienced; beings and things, the entire decor, too, combined in an unforgettable vision."[9]

But the time had not yet come to translate these impressions into images of his own creation. In the fall of 1862, Redon returned once more to Paris, this time in the hope of being admitted to the architecture section of the Ecole des Beaux-Arts. However, he failed in the oral examinations and went back to Bordeaux where for one year he studied with a sculptor and delighted in the handling of clay, although this material did not offer sufficient attraction to hold his interest. For a time the young man, liberated from the yoke of architecture, seems to have worked on his own, yet his production was slow and sparse. Eventually fate, which had already favored him in his first friendships, brought him still another one, the most significant of all, that of Rodolphe Bresdin, for some years stranded in Bordeaux. Then in his early forties, Bresdin was the typical Bohemian artist, oblivious to all practical matters of life, perpetually stricken with indigence, laboring with touching devotion in complete neglect, though never complaining nor losing his proud self-esteem.

13

He had already created an impressive number of lithographs, etchings, and pen and ink drawings, all black and white expressions of an essentially romantic and sometimes morbid imagination.

Bresdin's dilapidated studio, opposite a cemetery where Goya lay buried, became a place of daily pilgrimage for Redon, often accompanied by Clavaud. There they played music together, discussed science and philosophy, or endlessly debated the problems of art. Gorin and Clavaud (not to speak of Baudelaire) had confirmed Redon in his admiration for Delacroix. Now Bresdin revealed to him the greatness of Dürer and of Rembrandt, whom he revered above all. With profound gratitude Redon was to remember always the initiation he owed Bresdin. Once Gorin had helped him become conscious of his talent, it was Bresdin who offered Redon the guidance he needed, a guidance willingly accepted because it came not only from a generous heart but from a true artist whose passion and poverty, knowledge and vision put Redon in contact with genius and its burdens for the first time.

It was Bresdin—admirably suited for this role—who acquainted Redon with the strange process in which sensations derived from nature can be cast into images of utmost fancy. "His power," Redon subsequently explained, "lay in imagination alone. He never conceived anything beforehand. He improvised with joy, completing with tenacity the entanglements of the barely perceptible vegetation of the forests he dreamt up...."[10]

His new master warned the young man against all that was academic. While he himself completely eschewed the use of color, Bresdin was indignant that Ingres should have extolled the "probity" of draftsmanship. "Color is life itself," he told Redon. "It annihilates the line with its rays."[11] In his own works a curious maze of lines combined with subtle contrasts suggested these rays and contributed to the creation of an odd universe from which color was banned though not altogether absent. It was Bresdin who taught Redon the art of etching and of making lithographs which he called drawings on stone. One of Redon's first etchings, dated 1865, is signed "O. Redon, élève de Bresdin," and indeed the older man's influence is clearly apparent in his early endeavors in this medium (page 97). In some of the etchings of those days appear recollections of his excursion to the Pyrenees, others show those battle scenes or "evocations of scattered figures in rocky plains" which he had begun to draw (page 50) while Gorin had insisted on the objective study of nature.

Although work with a teacher of the caliber of Bresdin may have been pleasant enough, there can be little doubt that Redon was still plagued by the lack of certitude; his individuality emerged only slowly and obstinately refused to be hastened on its way. "My contemplative aptitude rendered painful my efforts towards a personal optic," he later confessed.[3] Since the arts of black and white do not seem to have completely satisfied him, he also painted occasionally and actually wondered whether he was born to be a colorist or a draftsman. One of his earliest attempts in oils, a small canvas of Arabs on horseback (page 51), shows him following in the footsteps of Delacroix. Yet he did not only venture into the field of imaginary scenes. With a friend who initiated him into the "sensualities of the palette" he went to paint landscapes in which he endeavored to seize the correct local colors.[3]

It may well be that Redon's father resigned himself to his son's vocation but—like the parents of Monet and Cézanne, for instance, whose sons were of the same age as Odilon—felt that he should at least study under the tutelage of an officially recognized master. By 1864, the young man was back in Paris where he became a pupil of Gérôme at the Ecole des Beaux-Arts. However, there was such a sharp contrast between the attitude of Gérôme and the warm interest and friendship with which Redon had been encouraged by Gorin and Bresdin, that his stay at the Ecole became a true ordeal.

"I paid a lot of attention to the rendering of form..."

Redon later reminisced. "I was prompted, in going to the Academy, by the sincere desire to place myself behind other painters, a pupil as they had been, and I expected from the others approval and justice. I did not take into account the art formula which was to guide me, and I was also forgetting my own disposition. I was tortured by the professor. Whether he recognized the sincerity of my serious inclination for study, or whether he saw in me a timid person of good will, he tried visibly to inculcate in me his own manner of seeing and to make me a disciple—or to make me disgusted with art itself. ... He exhorted me to confine within a contour a form which I myself saw as palpitating. Under pretext of simplification (and why?) he made me close my eyes to light and neglect the viewing of substances. ... The teaching I was given did not suit my nature. The professor had the most obscure and complete lack of appreciation of my natural gifts. He didn't understand anything about me. I saw that his obstinate eyes were closed before what mine saw. ... Young, sensitive, and irrevocably of my time, I was there hearing I-don't-know-what rhetoric, derived, one doesn't know how, from the works of the fixed past. ... No possible link between the two, no possible union; submission would have required the pupil's being a saint, which was impossible."[3]

Though still awkward and timid, Redon already obeyed an inner urge so strong that no outside influence could make him deviate from the road he had to follow. "One doesn't make the art one wants," he subsequently was to state,[3] and it is certainly true that even in the beginning he felt himself driven by creative necessities which would tolerate no compromises. Eagerness to learn was one thing, blind obedience another. Bresdin's rantings against academicism had ill prepared his young friend for the unimaginative routines of the Ecole des Beaux-Arts; they certainly now helped him withstand any encroachment on his emerging personality. It did not take Redon long to learn that he had nothing to learn from Gérôme. He apparently did not waste much time at the Ecole.

At the very moment when Gérôme failed him, Redon met another master whose example and work were to have a deep impact on him: Corot. Continuing in a certain sense—but with what authority!—the lessons given by Gorin, Corot stressed the balance that had to be established between imagination and observation. "Next to uncertainty always put a certitude,"[12] he told Redon, who understood that this meant contrasting vagueness with sharp detail. The advice Corot gave his young friend was to study nature with humility. "Go every year to paint at the same place, copy the same tree," he said.[12] Redon did not find it difficult to follow this recommendation, returning as he did periodically to Peyrelebade where he found himself in unison with nature and gathered new energy for work.

After the paroxysm of color he had admired in Delacroix, "the triumph of movement and passion over form,"[6] after the visions of a bizarre universe to which Bresdin had introduced him, Redon discovered in Corot's work delicate tonal values infused with poetic charm, a tender concept of nature seen through naive eyes. He gradually abandoned the meticulous pen and ink drawings of imaginary scenes which he had executed under Bresdin's influence (and also ceased, at least for some fifteen years, to produce any etchings). Instead, he began to use charcoal with its soft effects and subtle gradations, in which modulation replaces rigid lines, and thus absorbed the style that distinguishes the drawings of Corot's last years (page 51). When Redon used pencil, however, he often indulged in thin, linear shadings which appear related to the technique of engraving (page 53). But whatever technique he adopted, he did not abandon his predilection for imaginary subjects.

Redon seldom painted in those years. One of the rare oils of that period which has survived shows a rather sinister *Distributor of Laurel Wreaths*. Whether the idea for this strange and haunting canvas was suggested by

15

Redon: *The Distributor of Laurel Wreaths*. (Before 1870). Oil on paper, 16$\frac{1}{2}$ × 19$\frac{5}{8}$″. Collection Stephen Higgons, Paris

his hatred of officialdom (after all, he had failed in his attempt to earn laurels at the Ecole des Beaux-Arts) is hard to say. Redon himself later classed this painting among those "suggestive of allusions, innocently done. This work has the merit of being born in a time when nobody created with the brush that kind of expression or psychology."[13] Very early, it would seem, he became conscious of the fact that his attempts at self-expression kept him outside the general trends.

Often Redon went to the Louvre. He made drawings after Leonardo and Holbein, studied the delicate shapes of Tanagra figurines, copied a painting by Rembrandt, who always surprised and moved him anew because he gave "a moral life to the shadow."[14] Patiently he absorbed what the great masters of the past had to offer, though he never tried to follow them closely. He admitted that "Paris has its good sides, we speak badly of it yet it provides the artist with a direction for his effort,

an analysis of his self," but he nevertheless found it sometimes unbearable to live "far from the trees and unconscious nature."[15] At such moments a return to Peyrelebade became a necessity.

Redon continued to work quietly, without any hurry, but also without much energy. His frail constitution seems to have prevented him from strenuous endeavors. At the same time he sensed an undefinable conflict between his heart and his head and suffered from the difficulty of attaining the perfection of which he dreamt. By no means an idle "experimenter," he was hemmed in by the fear that he might not reach the desired peaks. But at least the inner forces which drove him on—groping and occasionally discouraged—did not impose on him a rhythm of haste or impatience. To the contrary, they seemed to demand a tardy gestation, and he readily gave in to their dictates, finding it easier to brood than to produce. "I am the child of my leisures," he once explained.[16] That he could abandon himself to such a slow-paced search for what he called his "optic" was possible because he did not have to be concerned with his livelihood. His family, no longer contradicting his disposition, gave him support sufficient for unstrained studies, and this in spite of the fact that since 1863, when phylloxera ravaged his vineyards, Redon's father had met with increasing difficulties in the administration of his properties. These reverses notwithstanding, the artist enjoyed even financially a pattern of life conducive to the slow budding of his genius. How much luckier he was than most of his contemporaries—Monet, Renoir, and Pissarro for instance—continuously engaged in the struggle of making a meager living while they pursued a highly unpromising career.

But during those early years in Paris Redon did more than visit the Louvre and abandon himself to introspective thoughts which he soon confided to a diary. He also acutely observed the contemporary scene and studied the new forces emerging in the art world. His "doleful and mystic soul" was sensitive to the social injustice and the abuses which incited Daumier, the greatest lithographer of the time, to his biting caricatures. Yet Redon, though "compassionate toward the disinherited of life,"[17] did not have the spirit of a fighter. If anything, his first contacts with reality after the sheltered existence he had led may have detached him from the Catholic Church, for like so many Frenchmen, he chose to believe in a divinity of his own, without benefit of clerical assistance.

More important to him were the events pertaining to art. It did not take him long to become aware of the stature of Courbet, then the rallying point for those who opposed the academic tyranny from which he himself had suffered for a short while. He also regularly inspected the official Salons despite the fact that a narrow-minded jury generally excluded all unconventional tendencies from these displays. He himself, in 1867, for the first time cleared the hurdle of this jury; it is true that he sent only a small etching to the print section of the Salon, the very etching on which he designated himself as "pupil of Bresdin." The following year, he again submitted a work to the jury, titled *Roland* (possibly the drawing reproduced on page 50), which was accepted but was apparently afterwards withdrawn by him, for it is not listed in the catalogue.

That same year, having just turned twenty-eight, he felt ready to send to *La Gironde*, a Bordeaux newspaper, a series of articles on the Salon of 1868 in which he summed up his own experiences and concepts. These articles, with their mature appraisals and their eloquent defence of imagination in art, a defense which went counter to the strong sweep of Courbet's realism and to the more recent emergence of Manet, show Redon ready to stand up for the convictions he had formed and to which he was to adhere thenceforth. Despite the indolence to which he had given in, it now became clear that his solitary and often wretched years in Paris had at last brought about a hard-won certitude and gained him the longed-for assurance.

Quite obviously, Redon had read Baudelaire's writings on art, which had helped him formulate his own position. He wholeheartedly agreed with the poet, who as early as 1859 had exclaimed: "From day to day art diminishes its self-respect, prostrates itself before exterior reality, and the artist becomes more and more inclined to paint not what he dreams but what he sees."[18] Redon's initial statement that the "great art" no longer existed sounds like an echo of Baudelaire's assertion, made more than twenty years before, that "the great tradition has been lost and the new one not yet been made."[19] But Redon did not simply draw from Baudelaire. He had personal things to say. The lucidity with which he evaluated, praised, or condemned the works exhibited was entirely his own. More important than the question of whether or not he was always right in his comments, was the fact that he now had found precepts by which to judge others and by which he could work himself. It was actually this last factor— the value of these precepts for his own endeavors—that endows his articles with particular interest.

"With some rare exceptions among the *genre* painters, one can say that the landscape school is today the honor of French painting," he wrote in his first article. He felt tempted to condemn the Salon altogether, but added that "the study of a few personalities already known and loved is still interesting enough and makes us forget this sad moment—doubtless a passing one— where the superior art, the human art is so disdainfully abandoned. Let us admit, the best things are still to be found among the works of artists who are seeking revitalization at the fecund sources of nature. Their impulse has been a salutary one."

Among the landscape painters it was Chintreuil, a pupil of Corot, whom Redon singled out for special praise, mostly because "he draws out, he anxiously, religiously explores all details—the procedure of the masters." Although he was not insensitive to Daubigny's attempts to reproduce the fleeting impression of a moment, Redon found his style too sketchy, not detailed enough. "One might think than an impression is incompatible with the feeling for form. M. Chintreuil, however, has succeeded in proving that the opposite is true: he has painted the shadow of a cloud cast on a meadow, at the same time scrupulously drawing the least flower. M. Daubigny does not wish to go so far. That is also the great defect of all those who have followed him in this, so to speak, fatal path: with the one word, Nature, much has been gained and much also forgotten. Some have been strong enough to find their personality in this direction, yet others, much more numerous, have lost the love of beauty, their respect for tradition. Under the pretext of being true, those qualities absolutely necessary to any beautiful work: modeling, character, arrangement, ampleness of planes, thought, philosophy, have been banned from painting."

Corot, in Redon's eyes, occupied a special position. In writing about him, he carefully avoided any allusion to his personal acquaintance with the master but did not resist repeating some of the advice he received from him. "Everybody knows," Redon said, "that M. Corot, whose paintings appear unfinished, is on the contrary extremely subtle and accomplished. . . . If, for the expression of his dreams, he intentionally leaves vague jumbles almost obliterated in semi-obscurity, he immediately places next to them a detail superbly firm and well observed. This proves clearly that the artist knows much; his dream is supported by a seen reality. . . . One asks oneself why M. Corot, who knows so well how to be a realist, always dares with great temerity to paint putti and nymphs. This is not the moment to open the eyes of those who insist upon restricting the painter's work to the reproduction of what he sees. Those who remain within these narrow limits commit themselves to an inferior goal. The old masters have proved that the artist, once he has established his own idiom, once he has taken from nature the necessary means of expression, is free, legitimately free, to borrow his sub-

jects from history, from the poets, from his own imagination, from the thousand sources of his fantasy. That makes the superior artist: face to face with nature he is a painter, but in his studio he is a poet and thinker."[20]

While Redon rated Corot as such a superior artist, he proceded, in his second article, to discuss men of the next and even of the most recent, that is his own generation. His choice was astounding, for among the five painters he elected to discuss as representative of a new

Redon: *Self Portrait*. (1867). Oil on wood, $16^{1}/_{8} \times 12^{5}/_{8}''$. Collection Arï Redon, Paris

approach were not merely Courbet and Manet, on whom much attention was then focused, but also three unknowns: Pissarro, Jongkind, and Monet. To have been so discerning as to acknowledge their originality, or at least their significance, in the maze of trivial canvases proposed by the Salon was in itself a major achievement which distinguishes Redon's comments from those of most professional critics of his day. Though Redon had made it quite clear that he did not overly appreciate the followers of Daubigny, he made an effort to be fair in his judgments. Thus he began by describing the general trend of the new movement (which was eventually to lead to impressionism):

"The aim is the direct reproduction of reality, to see nature and to render it attractive merely by faithfully copying it. If we grasp these tendencies, art here consists mainly in observing with as much naïveté as possible, in reproducing without intervention, without choice, without pre-established bias, without embellishment, as it were, leaving nature the master and the one responsible for the effect produced. The artist, then, must above all be supple and submissive before nature, obliterate the man so as to let the model shine." Courbet had this precious quality, Redon thought. In his early years, Courbet "boldly believing that he was renewing painting, declared himself eager for battle, ready to assume leadership of a school. But in his violent predilection for a return to nature, he exaggerated, selected from nature its most grotesque and ugly elements. There was loud laughter. The discernment necessary to see the salutary element in this return to something more true was missing. Yet art, declining because no longer sincere, needed rejuvenation."

"Today," Redon continued, "Courbet's work spreads with the fecundity of genuine power; he is chief of a school, and in this splendid triumph, which is legitimate, we wish to recall the complete frankness and force of his convictions."

Yet after this homage to the master and an extremely favorable analysis of one of his paintings, he voiced the objection that Courbet's position as head of a movement sometimes led him astray, hindering his "sincerity and possibly impeding the freedom of his sentiment. For it should be noted that his Salon entries always consist of one canvas composed of the sum of his talent, and another in which—less submissive to scruples—he obeys his platform rather than his own nature." Indeed, Redon objected to many of Courbet's figure compositions, which he found awkward, poorly assembled, almost vulgar. He concluded that Courbet was "a great colorist, his best qualities being amplitude, power, and delicacy. But what reservations must we make in regard to his tact and his taste!" Once more he insisted that Courbet's virtues could not wholly erase the "narrowness of the realist theories which confine art and refuse it access to its most fertile sources: thought, inspiration, genius—in a word—and all that it reveals to us."

Redon was much less receptive to the innovations of Manet, whom he put among Courbet's followers and considered extravagant and eccentric. Though conceding his originality, the newness and elegance of his colors, as well as his gift for harmony and his truly painterly talent, he considered Manet's masterful technique suited mostly for still lifes and landscapes. The portrait of Emile Zola, which Manet had sent to the Salon, prompted Redon to discuss the essential features of portraiture in general and to conclude:

"The weakness of M. Manet and of all those who, like him, want to limit themselves to the literal reproduction of reality, is to sacrifice man and his thought to good brush work, to the brilliant handling of a detail. The human being, for them, does not represent any more interest, any greater importance, than the beauty of his complexion or the picturesqueness of his attire. As a result their figures lack all moral life, that intimate and inner life which a painter translates in those felicitous moments when he expresses himself with particular intensity, possibly because he has seen and felt with profundity and vividness. It is on this point that true artists find themselves in decided opposition to paltry and restricted research. Although they recognize the necessity for a basis of *seen* reality, to them true art lies in a reality that is *felt*."

In spite of these reservations on the limitations of reality faithfully represented, Redon approached Pissarro's landscapes with particular sympathy. He praised his sincerity, his originality and restraint, but was less appreciative of Jongkind, whom he found too repetitive in subject and technique. Whereas Redon recognized Monet's audacity, he reproached him for having treated his landscape on too large a scale. In concluding, Redon regretted the absence of Millet who, "more sagacious than the others, does not disregard the counsel of tradition. Not disdaining to study the masters, he has discerned what he could derive from them in simplicity, sobriety, and search for style, qualities which the painters whose works we have just examined do not have. ... We must remember that we have other things than the eyes to satisfy, that we carry in ourselves ... troubles, joys, or pains to which the great artist knows how to address himself."[21]

In his third and last article, Redon repeated again that beyond reality "blindly reproduced" there exists another way, "less precise and yet just as true, less external but more intimate and concentrated, which consists in expressing—with the aid of all the elements that nature offers—a human action, a sentiment, and in inserting this sentiment into the landscape, explaining it, commenting on it, so to speak, through local color, through the aspect of the sky, the day, the moment."

This ultimate article was devoted to the *genre* painters and afforded Redon an opportunity to pay a debt of gratitude to Bresdin, "a little known artist, but dear to a rare few, who pursues on sheets not larger than a hand all the best characteristics of true art. ... He proposes to the world, perhaps for the future, pages in which can be found the real conditions for durability:

talent, imagination, sincere reflection of inner feeling."

Using the subject of *genre* painting for a further exploration of the role of imagination in art, Redon chose Eugène Fromentin (author of a psychological novel as well as painter) to make his point. Pleading for the legitimacy of pictorial invention, he called it "a right that has been lost and which we must reconquer: the right to fantasy, to the free interpretation of history. The example of the great artists of the past justifies this claim. If, in order to convince the most rebellious ones, it does not suffice to state that this truth imposes itself today [with the work of Fromentin] ... if the entire collection of the Louvre with its masterpieces, and the clarity of their language, is not a protest strong and solemn enough, then we shall have to wait patiently until the light dawns. We shall have to tell those who are the most misled to bide their time a little longer, to listen sincerely and with more veneration to the noble language of beauty. The moment will come without doubt. Maybe it will be given to those who are still in the somber anteroom to lift a corner of the veil, to see at last, beyond the penumbra, in the splendor of a luminous clearing, this beautiful garden of poetry, filled with great murmuring and delights. It is a homeland made for all. How many pure joys they abjure who obstinately limit art!"[22]

In writing his articles, Redon was not so much attracted by art criticism (which he considered sterile unless it concerned itself with tendencies and ideas) as he was prompted by the desire to apply to contemporary art what he had learned in the Louvre, derived from the observation of new trends and, above all, gained from probing into his soul. He may have considered himself one of those who were still in that "somber anteroom," ready to lift a corner of the veil, and certainly had described his own condition when he proclaimed in his last article: "What makes the strength of the artist, what makes his greatness, his supreme superiority, is precisely an anxious timidity, submission, and appre-

20

hension attentive to the secret indications of the ideal." Whereas he could not yet claim superiority for himself, he did know all the pangs of those who eagerly wait for the hidden manifestations of their ideal. The main thing was that he had found his ideal, and that he was conscious of the direction in which he was headed.

Apparently the enunciation of his concepts did not encourage Redon to more sustained efforts. Early in 1870 he complained to Gorin that he had "suffered much during the last year," whereupon his former teacher reminded him that he was now old enough to make a place for himself in the art world, but that only ample and determined production could help him achieve this goal.[23] At least he was kept busy during the spring and early summer of 1870, when an architect friend requested his help with the mural decorations of a chapel in Arras.[24] This work, for which Redon sought inspiration in the murals of Puvis de Chavannes, bolstered his confidence, though it did not put an end to his uneasy introspection.

This peculiar type of self-torment was interrupted in July 1870 by the declaration of the Franco-Prussian War. Redon returned to Bordeaux where the new republican government, created after the fall of the Second Empire, established itself. In October, he was drafted. And a strange thing happened: the tragic conflict which took such a disastrous turn for France had an invigorating effect on the artist, so wholly unprepared for martial experiences. He had always considered himself frail and now to his surprise discovered that he was able to stand the rigors of a soldier's life, to stand them well, and even to enjoy them. This he said later on many occasions. Moreover, the war—brutally putting a halt to his disquieting meditations—confronted him with new concerns, with problems of physical danger, of fighting, and of death. Although he evidently abhorred the idea of having to kill and was by no means a fanatical patriot, he wore his uniform without reluctance. With deep curiosity he registered all happenings and describ-

ed them in exalted letters to his family. These letters are lost but a reply sent by his brother Ernest on the last day of December 1870 seems to follow in detail Redon's reports from the front:

"You are gallant, dear Odilon. Your letters surprise us. We can't get over your courage, your composure. For it does take these, and even a strong dose of them, to be able to observe as you have done and to give me (the musician, and for this I thank you) all that curious information on the various sounds made by projectiles. Your last letter from Saumur is charming and very precious. . . ."[25]

Redon always maintained that the war made him *will* (these were his words), that it made him conscious of his natural gifts, and even cast a new light on his previous efforts. "The least important sketches or scribbles which I had left in my portfolios now had a meaning in my eyes."[1]

Redon eventually fell ill and, towards the end of January 1871, was released from the Army for "general weakness, result of fever." He was back in Bordeaux or probably at Peyrelebade when the peace was signed in May and the *Commune* bloodily suppressed in Paris. A little later he returned to the capital, determined now to immerse himself in his art. Detached though he was by then from Bresdin's influence, in one point at least he followed his example: he restricted himself to a black and white medium—charcoal, however, rather than pen and ink. Actually his charcoal drawings were not precisely black and white (he liked to call them "my blacks") since he frequently did them on paper of pale brown, yellow, rose, or blue, providing them with a "promise of color."

Although Redon had been elated by his short military experience, it was under the sign of sadness that he now entered upon a new and decisive phase, for as he noted in his diary: "Of all moral situations most favorable for producing art or thought, there are none that are more fecund than great patriotic griefs."[26] It seems idle to speculate what direction his work might have taken, had France emerged from the war victorious, but if Redon really needed sorrow to be stimulated, a merciful fate once more provided it. As a matter of fact, he did not require any specific motif for unhappiness, and he openly admitted that sadness, even "when it comes without cause, is perhaps a secret fervor, a kind of prayer said confusedly for some function in the unknown."[27] Moreover, he now had cause for worry, since it looked as though he might have to earn his living. For a while he considered working as a violinist in an orchestra to support himself, yet he appears to have been able, at least for a few more years, to concentrate on his work.

Inspired by the afflictions which gripped his country, and haunted by the oppressive memories of his youth, he set about confiding to lightly tinted sheets all the besetting images which seemed to yearn for a permanent form. The technique he developed, while thoroughly personal, showed a vague similarity to the style of Millet's drawings, one of the few artists who were then using charcoal to establish softly modeled dark masses against gentle areas of brightness. According to Redon's own words, what attracted him to this medium was the fact that "charcoal, a volatile matter which can be lifted by a breath, granted me the rapidity of a gestation conducive to the docile and easy expression of my feelings."[27]

He discovered that "the heavy and vital ardor charcoal gives depends on the fullness of physical energy,"[27] the very energy which only since the war he knew he possessed. But above all he found that "it carries the vitality of the artist, his mind, something of his soul, the reflection of his sensitivity, a residue which belongs to him and to the medium."[27] Eventually he was to exclaim with enthusiasm: "One must respect black. Nothing prostitutes it. It does not please the eye or awaken another sense. It is the agent of the mind even more than the beautiful color of the palette or prism."[27] This fer-

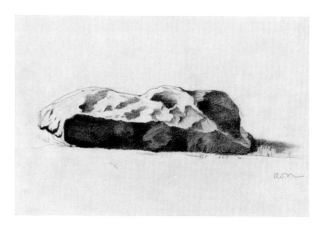

Redon: *Stone.* (1870–75). Pencil, 5 × 11″. Collection Arï Redon, Paris

Redon: *Basement at Peyrelebade.* (c. 1870). Pencil, 9½ × 8½″. Collection Arï Redon, Paris

22

vent declaration notwithstanding, Redon was to elevate black precisely to a level where it became pleasing to the eye and where it did awaken another sense, that of the supernatural.

As he submerged himself in his work, he came to realize the extent to which he lacked any formal training (some of his early drawings are awkward and angular). He once more returned to the Louvre to consult the classic masters. From time to time he also went to the Faculty of Medicine for the study of anatomy, or to the Museum of Natural History to acquire a proper knowledge of osteology. Indeed, his desire to provide the fantastic beings that populated his dreams with a "visual logic" drove him to the most careful exploration of human and animal structure, of nature in general, which he had so often neglected. His aim, which he had already enunciated in his Salon reviews of 1868, was to interlock intimately in his mind and work reality *felt* and reality *observed*. He explained their peculiar relationship when he wrote: "I have always felt the need to copy nature in small objects, particularly the casual or accidental. It is only after making an effort of will to represent with minute care a grass blade, a stone, a branch, the face of an old wall, that I am overcome by the irresistible urge to create something imaginary. External nature, thus assimilated and measured, becomes —by transformation—my source, my ferment. To the moment following such exercises I owe my best works."[3]

Strange as it may seem, Redon's imaginary drawings were not made in "exile" in Paris, where he might conceivably have called upon memories that would have transported him back to the haunts of his youth. His charcoal drawings—some six hundred of them—originated at Peyrelebade, "in the complete isolation of the country." He returned there every summer, impregnated himself with its peacefulness and labored in the fields until physical effort brought about "a certain productive ebullition in the brain. How many times," he once said, "have I taken charcoal into my hands

soiled with earth!"[27] The summers in that region are heavy with tremendous thunderstorms that seem to set the countryside afire. In autumn dense fogs appear which, as they lift, are succeeded by a singularly transparent atmosphere.[28] Occasionally the artist painted some small, tender landscapes there.

Redon always insisted that his imagination had its roots in the observation of nature. To him even the most fantastic drawings were "true" because the visions he translated into the velvet-like texture of charcoal drawings were never absolutely detached from reality; they were part of his own world, of his peculiar atavism. As he has said: "My originality consists in bringing to life, in a human way, improbable beings and making them live according to the laws of probability, by putting—as far as possible—the logic of the visible at the service of the invisible."[3]

Thus was born that bizarre universe of improbable creatures vested with a life of their own, breathing, despite their grotesque abnormalities, according to secret laws which no Darwin could discover but which a solitary genius established on the basis of his unerrring imagination. There were eyes floating in the air similar to immense balloons, heads ascending into space, carried by their ears shaped like the wings of bats, flowers with melancholy faces emerging from the marshlands, gruesome polyps with forlorn grins, eggs resembling bald heads emptily staring from outsized cups, spiders that smiled and spiders that wept, skulls among ruins and skeletons with bare branches sprouting from their domes, deathly pale masks growing on trees, cactuses with human features, bristling with thorns, orbs enigmatically shining among dark tree trunks, worms ending in one-eyed balls (pages 56–61). True, there was also every now and then the sweet face of a child, the delicate profile of a woman, her loveliness accentuated by subtle shading; but more often than not, the humans which appeared undisguised in Redon's drawings were shown in sinister or unusual contexts: as prisoners crouching behind bars; clad in strange armors with forbidding spikes; surrounded by menacing reptiles.

Where did they come from? Can the clouds and the gnarled trees, the sad peasants, the owls and the crumbling walls which impressed Redon as a sensitive child, can they have suggested all these apparitions? Some were to liken the artist to Goya whose work Redon evidently knew and admired. But Goya's imagination was generally linked to his attitude of social and religious protest. It was a function of his bitter, ironic, and vibrant message. A realist engaged wholeheartedly in the fight against despotism and cruelty, Goya resorted to satire and grotesqueness as a medium to make himself heard, to comment bitingly on the wickedness of his times. His originality and power lay precisely in the mastery with which he made his imagination serve the high purpose of his anger. Yet there is no anger, no sarcasm, no revolt, no wish to ridicule existing institutions behind the creations of Redon; they are an exploration of an enigmatic beyond for its own sake, for the sake of their purely plastic portents.[29]

Others were to compare Redon to his contemporary, Gustave Moreau, although Moreau's monsters never leave the path of tradition. His centaurs and hydras, unicorns and sphinxes, cyclops and vultures are derived from classic sources and usually have a definite role, that of enhancing the evil beauty of libidinous virgins, unless they help intensify the remarkable purity of superb young heroes of legends. Redon, on the other hand, seldom addressed himself to antiquity for inspiration, though Phaeton and Pegasus appear in his works. His freaks do not present themselves in lusciously defined settings that underline their fiendishness. He did not have to resort to any oppositions between the unlikely and the likely in order to stress the strangeness of his imaginings. His visions exist by themselves, in an independent sphere over which they reign absolutely. They are an end, not a means for the sake of obvious contrasts. They are a necessity imposed upon

him by the inescapable urge of his fantasy.

He was often asked to explain the meaning of his drawings, and much as Redon liked to dwell on his childhood reminiscences or to probe into the sources of his inspiration, he found it difficult to reply to such inquiries. He experienced the same difficulties when he was requested to reveal how he actually worked. But when, in 1898, his friend Mellerio prepared an essay on him, he felt it would be ungracious to avoid the issue and told him: "I can't answer you completely. What interest do you find in knowing whether I approach the easel or the lithographic stone under the guidance of a pre-established concept? For thirty years I have been asked that question. You won't believe how much it embarrasses me; I never replied. What is the use of revealing other things than the result?... However, I can confide in you, if you wish, some invincible particularities of my nature. Thus a sheet of white paper horrifies me. It impresses me disagreeably to the point of making me sterile, of depriving me of the taste for work (except, of course, when I propose to represent a real object, for example a study or a portrait). A sheet of paper is so shocking to me that I am forced, as soon as it is on the easel, to scrawl on it with charcoal, with a crayon or any other material, and this operation brings it to life. I believe that suggestive art owes much to the stimulus which the material itself exerts on the artist. A truly sensitive artist does not receive the same inspiration from different materials since these impress him differently. This will make you understand that the pre-established concept of which you speak acts only indirectly and relatively. Frequently it is, without doubt, like a departure for the undertaking, a departure which one abandons in due course to follow the charming and unforeseen path of fantasy, that sovereign which suddenly opens up before us magnificent and surprising seductions by which we are subjugated. This fantasy has been my guardian angel.

"Fantasy is also the messenger of the 'unconscious,'

24

of that very eminent and mysterious personage . . . who arrives in his own time, according to the moment, the place, even the season. This should enlighten you and make you understand how difficult it is to answer the 'why' or 'how,' since in the fatal crucible in which the the work of art is wrought, everything is dominated by the precious caprice of that unknown. . . . Nothing in art is achieved by will alone. Everything is done by docilely

Redon: *Chimera*. (1902). Charcoal, $21^5/_8 \times 15^1/_4''$. Collection Mrs. A. Bonger, Almen, The Netherlands

submitting to the arrival of the 'unconscious.' The analytical spirit must be quick when it appears, but afterwards it is of little importance to remember it, as with each work it proposes a different problem to us."[30]

While Redon felt that it was better to "hide a little" the stimulus which brought about the extraordinary images he created (as if to divulge his secret might have angered the "mysterious personage" that guided him), he was always willing to explain by which means he achieved his fantastic drawings. With "conscious maturity," as he put it, he insisted that his art was "limited uniquely to the resources of chiaroscuro and also owed much to the effects of abstract line, that agent of profound sources which acts directly on the mind. Suggestive art cannot give anything without exclusive recourse to the mysterious play of shadows and to the rhythm of mentally conceived lines." But he added that the artist's nature also had something to say, since it prescribes "obedience to the gifts with which it endowed us. Mine have induced me to dreams; I have sustained the torments of imagination and the surprises with which it steered my pencil. Yet I directed and led these surprises according to the laws of an art which I know, which I feel, and I have done this for the sole purpose of involving the spectator, by means of a sudden attraction, in all the allure of the uncertain. . . ." And Redon elaborated that "suggestive art is most independently and most radiantly present in the exciting sounds of music, but it is also mine through a combination of various associated elements, forms transposed and transformed, without any relation to contingencies, yet having their own logic. . . . My drawings *inspire* yet cannot be defined. They do not determine anything. Like music, they transport us into the ambiguous world of the undetermined."[3]

The important thing, as Redon said, was the result, the organic work of art, no matter where its components came from. That he could achieve these results was due to the fact that he did not "invent" his subjects but

25

actually saw them with his mind's eye while simultaneously recording them in a purely pictorial language. Not to break the mysterious spell of his inspiration, to submit to it without losing control, that was the problem which in every new work confronted him. Whether he borrowed some symbols from literature, whether he was stimulated by the concerts he faithfully attended, whether he fell back on distant memories or obeyed the dictate of an urgent impression, he never "translated" ideas from one medium into another; he transcribed directly what appeared to him. The images which emerged, after the first lines on the virgin paper had provoked the effusion of his fantasy, took shape according to their own *logic* (a word which Redon cherished), they were not equivalents or approximations, they were the immediate expression of a pure, plastic concept whose manifold sources paled before the exigencies of creation. It is not surprising, then, that Redon hardly bothered to investigate their meaning and preferred vague, ambiguous titles for his works, since his object was to exteriorize and communicate his visions rather than to impart a message.

Behind these visions undeniably lay an obsession with supernatural and menacing forces. Only rarely did his fantasy suggest pleasant or appeasing vistas to him. But his gruesome or sad specters do not appear to be the result of exasperation or frustation. Escaping from the world of reality into that of somber dreams which held such a deep attraction for him, he merely followed the bent of his own nature that since childhood had prepared his solitary and sensitive soul for the association with shadows. Later on he was to prove in exquisitely chaste nudes and in lovely arrangements of flowers that his inclinations were by no means warped, that he was sensitive to the charms of nature. Yet before he could approach more felicitous subjects, he apparently had to set free the strange apparitions which had haunted him for years. And whatever he read,

from *Hamlet* to the *Divine Comedy*, seemed to stimulate him further to explore the mysterious realm of darkness.[31]

One of his favorite authors, Pascal, whose *Pensées* he never put aside for long, once even inspired him with the desire to illustrate his maxims, although he soon gave up this almost impossible task. It was in Pascal that he found a thought which also deeply impressed Gustave Moreau: "Human knowledge is similar to a sphere which ceaselessly grows as its volume increases, thus enlarging its points of contact with the unknown." This seems to describe exactly his own situation, except that in Redon's case the steadily extending contiguity with the unfathomable attracted rather than upset him. He was in the unique position of deriving inspiration both from the known and from the unknown.

In distinct contrast to his charcoal drawings which served his quest for the unknown, Redon's minute studies from nature were usually drawn with a pencil whose sharpness permitted greater attention to detail. Pencil drawings not only led him to imaginary creations, they also constituted a "repertory" which he was to consult frequently, so that certain forms of trees, for instance, reappear throughout his work, often in different media. They were private notes which had their usefulness both in order to bring about the state of mind required for the exploration of the invisible and to establish a ready frame of reference for his concern with the visible. But it was in his charcoal drawings that Redon addressed himself to an as yet nonexisting audience. He submitted "humbly to the responsibility of cultivating one's faculties for the pleasure of reaping and sharing the results with those who wait to accept them."[27] The trouble was that nobody seemed to wait, and his attempts to exhibit his "blacks" at the yearly Salon appear to have been thwarted by the jury. Yet, strangely enough, the artist never specifically complained about the isolation in which he labored during the years after the war. What may have affected him more was the fact that among his few friends, his confidant Clavaud and his former master Gorin were unable to follow his evolution. However, his road being firmly traced by now, their lack of understanding could not change the course of things; Redon loyally maintained his devotion to them.

In 1874 Bresdin left for Canada. His ties with Redon, already somewhat loosened, were now interrupted for some time. That same year, Redon's propensity for sadness was sustained by the death of his father, whom he mourned with a tinge of regret for not having been closer to him. His grief was deepened by the fact that this loss also menaced the survival of Peyrelebade. Indeed, the estate—undivided among the heirs—was thenceforth administered by the artist's brothers who knew little about such matters and who, together with their mother, concerned themselves primarily with revenues where Redon saw only sentimental attachments. For more than twenty years he had to live under their threat to sell the property, increasingly burdened with mortgages, a threat which to him was unbearable since Peyrelebade symbolized the very roots of his inspiration. Although he continued to spend his summers there, the endless disputes involving financial questions became a source of suffering for the artist. Eventually he lost all contact with his family and saw the warm

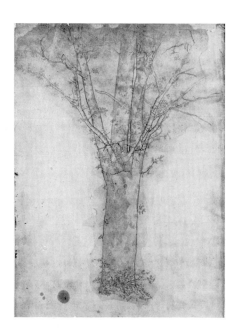

Redon: *Tree*. (c.1892). Pencil, 18⁵/₈ × 12¹/₂″. Collection Jere Abbott, Dexter, Maine

Redon: *Tree*. (1892). Lithograph, 18³/₄ × 12⁵/₈″. The Art Institute of Chicago. The Stickney Fund

Redon: *Buddha*, (decorative panel). (1904). Collection Mrs. A. Bonger, Almen, The Netherlands

Redon: *Cyclops.* 1883. Lithograph, $8^7/_{16} \times 7^{13}/_{16}''$. The Museum of Modern Art. Gift of Victor S. Riesenfeld

Redon: *Cyclops.* (c. 1880). Pencil, $4^5/_8 \times 6^1/_4''$. Private collection, New York

cordiality which had existed between him and his brother Ernest replaced by bitter enmity. He also now had to give up the modest income he had received. It is not known how he managed to earn the little he needed for his frugal life, except that around 1878 a Paris dealer agreed to sell his "blacks," though it has not been recorded whether or not he was successful.

At the very time these events cast their shadows over his existence, Redon found himself admitted to a new and congenial circle. At the weekly gatherings which he regularly attended after 1874 in the house of Madame de Rayssac, a hostess of unusual charm and brilliance, he met a group of writers, artists, and musicians among whom he felt singularly at ease. He did not speak much, preferring to listen, especially to recollections of Delacroix or if problems of poetry were discussed. When music was being played, he modestly turned the pages of the score. He met the composer Ernest Chausson there, not yet twenty, with whom he formed a solid friendship. Every Saturday he went to Chausson's house, the musician playing the piano while Redon accompanied him on the violin. Schumann was their god.

At Madame de Rayssac's Redon also became acquainted with Fantin-Latour who revealed to him a new technique of making lithographs. Bresdin always had drawn directly on cumbersome lithographic stones and had done so with a pen, a tool hostile to tenebrous evocations. Fantin-Latour now directed Redon's attention to a special paper on which one could draw with a lithographic crayon, and from which the finished drawing could be transferred mechanically on stone. In this way the transfer and the printing could be done by technicians, and the artist relieved of the more tedious aspects of the lithographic process. Redon was immediately attracted by this technique in which he found a means to "multiply" his drawings but which he eventually came to like for its own sake. Lithography soon became an essential form of expression for him. His first album of prints, significantly called *Dans le rêve* and composed

28

of lithographs which had no thematic link with each other—created as they were after charcoal drawings made at Peyrelebade—appeared in 1879.

More important still, Redon met at Madame de Rayssac's a young girl, Camille Falte, born on the French island of Bourbon near Madagascar in the Indian Ocean, who on May 1, 1880 became his wife (page 55). Their union was to be a completely happy and cloudless one. She shared his taste for discretion and calm, accepted without complaint the hardships of life with an as yet unknown artist, and took charge of such practical matters as discussions with publishers and dealers. The home she prepared for him was pervaded by an atmosphere of quiet cheerfulness such as he had never known before and which he enjoyed the more as it did not interfere with his melancholy inclinations. Above all, Madame Redon stood by his side in the harrowing struggle for Peyrelebade, in what he called "the most tragic though occult hours of my family drama." Some twenty years after their wedding Redon was to say: "Without her, and also without the shades of black which I have unrolled and poured on paper, what would have become of me! My art alone, so deep inside, would not have been sufficient to save me—I was lost! I believe that the *yes* which I pronounced the day we were united was the expression of the most complete and unadulterated certitude I have felt. A certitude more absolute even than that of my vocation."[32]

Two years before his marriage Redon had spent some time in Brittany where he had first stayed during his convalescence as a soldier. He returned there again in 1883. He made pencil drawings and painted some small landscapes there (page 54) which still show the ascendency of Corot but in which there is a sense for structure and for simplified, sometimes bold forms. Delicacy of color is combined with a forceful division of light and dark areas, of summarized shapes, which foretell the endeavors the Nabis were to make some ten years later. Yet landscape painting was for Redon a relaxation rather than an end in itself, a venture into the realm of color which still held few temptations for him. Had he not noted in his diary, after visiting the fourth group exhibition of the mercilessly ridiculed impressionists in 1880, that the approach of these artists was a very legitimate one "when applied mainly to the representation of external objects under the open sky. However, I do not believe that all which palpitates under the brow of a man who meditates and listens to his inner voices—nor do I believe that *thought*, taken for itself—can gain much from this tendency of observing only what is happening outside of our walls. On the contrary, the expression of life can appear but in chiaroscuro. Thinkers prefer the shade, stroll through it, are at ease in it, as if their brains found their natural element there. All well considered, these very worthy painters do not sow particularly rich fields in the domain of art. 'Man is a thinking being.' Man will always be there; whatever the role played by light, it won't be able to turn him aside. To the contrary, the future belongs to a subjective world."[33]

These concepts, already expressed in his articles of 1868, had been fortified when Redon, in 1878, went to Holland for the special purpose of studying Rembrandt's works. He marvelled at the discovery that, while certain biblical subjects and certain details of his compositions belong "to literature and even to philosophy, one feels very well that all this plays only the role of an accessory and that the artist, in a willed or unconscious endeavor, did not make of these elements the unique condition of his pictures." The real accent of his paintings lay in their supernatural light. "There, in the pure and simple nature of the tone, in the delicacies of chiaroscuro, is the secret of the entire work, a completely picturesque invention which incarnates the idea and gives it flesh and bones, so to speak. This has nothing to do with anecdotes."[34] Redon was less taken by Rubens, although he acknowledged in him the precursor of Delacroix and other painters who "express the life of things much more by reflecting exterior nature in their memories than through the observation and immediate analysis of the model."[34] However, this excursion into Holland had no specific consequences, except that the enthusiastic examination of Rembrandt's etchings in Amsterdam may have caused Redon to return with renewed ardor to his own work.

Redon was past forty when, a few years later, in 1881, he held his first modest one-man show, composed mostly of charcoal drawings, on the premises of the weekly *La Vie Moderne* which did not even bother to advertise the event in its pages. The exhibition did not dent the wall of indifference with which the general public always seems to protect itself against innovators who threaten to disturb its habits of seeing and thinking. The artist was naively surprised by this attitude of "coldness and reserve which will remain in my memory as an enigma."[35] It is true that Huysmans, already well-known though still in the orbit of Zola's then powerful "naturalism," took notice of the exhibition and hastily appended, apropos of Gustave Doré, a few lines to his Salon review:

"Another artist, painter of the fantastic, has recently come to the fore in France; I refer to M. Odilon Redon. Here is the nightmare transported into art. If you intermingle, in gruesome surroundings, somnambulistic figures that have a vague affinity with those of Gustave Moreau, though transfixed by terror, you may perhaps get an idea of the bizarre talent of this singular artist."[36]

The following year, Redon once more exhibited a group of drawings and lithographs, this time in the offices of a newspaper, *Le Gaulois*. The public laughed openly at his creations, but Huysmans' sensitive imagination was fired by their contemplation. It led him to speak of "animalcules of vinegar swarming in glucose tinted with soot," and of a "fetus by Correggio macerated in a bath of alcohol." Huysmans concluded: "It would be difficult to define the surprising art of M. Redon. Basically, if we except Goya, whose spectral

Redon: *Street in Quimper, Brittany*. (c. 1880). Oil on cardboard, 12³/₈ × 9″. Collection Arï Redon, Paris

side is less rambling and more real, if we also except Gustave Moreau, of whom M. Redon is, after all, in the healthy parts of his work, a very distant pupil, we shall find his ancestry only among musicians perhaps, and certainly among poets. It is indeed a genuine transposition of one art into another. The masters of this artist are Baudelaire and especially Edgar Poe, whose consoling aphorism that *all certitude lies in dreams* he appears to have pondered."[37] In speaking of the "healthy" parts of Redon's works, Huysmans seemed to imply that there were also unhealthy ones, yet he had nevertheless intuitively linked the artist with music, with Baudelaire, with Poe.

Later that same year, Redon was to publish his second album of lithographs, dedicated to the American writer, although Poe was not really his favorite author. Redon did not agree with Huysmans' interpretation of his monsters as being indebted to the "microscope confronting the frightful world of the infinitesimal" and jotted down: "No. When I created them, I had the more important concern of organizing their structures."[3] Just the same, he was "singularly happy and proud" to have been noticed by Huysmans. Soon, the latter wrote directly to Redon: "You will doubtless be greatly surprised to see that a naturalist writer should conceive such a passion for your delectable and so cruelly fantastic works."[38] Whereupon Huysmans went to see the artist who was captivated by his charm. A precious friendship was born.

The truth is that Huysmans was no longer a "naturalist writer." He discovered Redon at the very moment when he began work on a new novel, *Against the Grain*, which was to detach him completely from Zola and to herald a new literary movement, that of Symbolism.[39] One of his friends later went so far as to say that it was in part his association with Redon and Moreau that had revived Huysmans' "propensity for the immaculate dream, a tendency towards evasive flights from the present."[40] Bent on shattering the limits of the novel, on opening it to art, science, and history, while concentrating on the single figure of his decadent hero, des Esseintes, Huysmans included long passages on Redon and Moreau in his new book, describing their works in purely literary terms that seemed more revealing of his own imagination than of the tendencies of the two artists of whom he spoke so glowingly. Thus he wrote of Redon's drawings that they were "outside of any known category; most of them leap beyond the boundaries of painting, innovating a very special fantasy, a fantasy of sickness and delirium."[41]

But Redon's small exhibition of 1882 also brought him the admiration of a critic who was able to judge his work on its inherent artistic merits rather than on the basis of fanciful interpretations, Moved by his drawings, Emile Hennequin paid a visit to the artist and published a long article on him. "From now on," he said, "M. Odilon Redon should be considered one of our masters and—for those who value above all this touch of strangeness without which, according to Francis Bacon, there is no exquisite beauty—as an outstanding master who, Goya excepted, has no ancestors or emulators. He has suceeded in conquering, somewhere on the border between reality and fantasy, a desolate domain which he has peopled with formidable ghosts, monsters, monads, composite beings made of every possible human perversity, bestial baseness, and of all kinds of terrors of inert and noxious things. . . . As much as Baudelaire, M. Redon deserves the superb praise of having created '*un frisson nouveau.*'

"His work is bizarre; it touches the grandiose, the delicate, the subtle, the perverse, the seraphic. . . . It contains a treasure of dreams and suggestions which should be used cautiously. Add to its idealism an astounding mastery of execution which makes all these lithographs and drawings appear more luminous and more powerful than etchings, an impeccable draftsmanship which forces the eye to accept even the strangest deformations of real beings, and one realizes that such works can arouse admiration."[42]

Redon was deeply touched by this appreciation and immediately wrote Hennequin: "It is my turn to congratulate you warmly. First to express the joy which reading what you think about my works has given me; but also to compliment you vigorously on the courage that you have shown. Allow me to tell you also that criticism is a form of creation like any other and that in some way you have just collaborated with me, the solitary, on my work. Thank you. The help which you generously and with so much sympathy have brought me dissipates much of my anguish and I feel myself nobler, now that I can continue to work for young spirits. . . ."[43]

Contact with youth became one of Redon's hopes. It may have been his desire to come in closer touch with young artists that prompted Redon, in 1884, to participate in the founding of the *Société des Artistes Indépendants* which, in opposition to the official Salon, abolished any type of jury and opened the doors of its yearly exhibitions to all comers.[44] Redon benevolently presided over the agitated meetings of the new association, of which he accepted the vice-presidency. He exhibited with the Independents in 1884, 1886, and 1887, after which he abstained, probably because his works were buried by an avalanche of mediocrity that only Seurat, Signac, and their friends were able to brave since they presented themselves as a coherent group.

Redon remained a figure aloof, although the rising Symbolist movement slowly began to create the climate in which he could be appreciated. When Huysmans introduced the artist to Mallarmé, Redon—so susceptible to music, be it that of words or sounds—met at last the one poet whom he understood and admired completely. What these two lonely geniuses felt for each other was more than friendship; they became brothers whose mutual affection was enriched by a deep, a total respect.

The warmth and sincerity of Mallarmé's comprehension outdistanced by far that of many other Symbolist writers whose praise sprang less from a profound esteem for Redon's work than from approval of his tendencies, in which the Symbolists saw many parallels to their own literary endeavors. It is not surprising, then, that the artist felt a little awkward in the midst of his new admirers, unable to satisfy them with the precepts and theories of which they were so fond. "I am supposed to have much more of an analytical mind than I really have," Redon confided to his diary; "this would at least account for the curiosity that I feel in the young writers who visit me. In contact with me I see them at first somewhat surprised. What did I put into my work to suggest so much subtlety? I placed in it a little door opening on mystery. I made fiction. It is for them to go further."[45]

Redon's visitors apparently expected the author of so many disquieting images to be a somewhat sinister or tormented figure. After calling upon the artist, Signac once jotted down that he had met "masses of people trailing into Redon's studio, thinking he may prove to be a queer fellow easy to exploit, or a bluffer with whom one might associate. They lose no time in disappearing when they find him merely a good and simple maker of black-and-whites."[46]

Indeed, those who came to see him discovered Redon to be modest and friendly, a middle-aged man of quiet bearing, unassuming, and with none of the characteristics of the "artist," his manners polite and soft, always discoursing gently and tolerantly, though firm in his refusal to discuss the "meaning" of his works. "In the beginning," he later stated, "all the errors committed by the critics on my behalf resulted from the fact that they did not see that there was nothing to be defined, nothing to be understood . . . because all that is sincerely and docilely new carries . . . its significance in itself."[3]

What could the young writers and other visitors learn from an artist who directed them to look at his work (as Mallarmé did devotedly) rather than explain it to them? Yet it was deeply satisfying to Redon that his name was now pronounced with increasing frequency and respect, a circumstance for which Huysmans, despite the shortcomings of his too literary approach, was mainly responsible and for which Redon was grateful to him. The appearance of Huysmans' novel *Against the Grain* in 1884 revealed Redon and Mallarmé to a public that had ignored them. This public, not a very large one, it is true, was tired of Zola's painstaking and down to earth descriptions, of the "compulsorily contemporaneous," and eager, instead, for symbols, sensa-

32

tions, and ideas, for an art that derived "from objectivity only a simple and extremely succinct point of departure."[47]

Two factors, the happy life he was now leading with his recent bride and the attention that began to be focused on his work, contributed to Redon's expanded activity in the early eighties. Yet sorrows continued to cross his path. In November 1884 a younger brother died of consumption at the age of thirty-three, followed into the grave, a few weeks later, by their only sister. Meanwhile Redon's albums of lithographs succeeded themselves in rapid sequence, attesting to an almost feverish creativity. *À Edgar Poë* of 1882 was followed in 1883 by *Les origines*, by *Hommage à Goya* in 1885 (for which Mallarmé wrote the artist an exquisite letter of thanks[48]), and by *La nuit* in 1886. Many of these plates were conceived specifically for the lithographic stone which had, as Redon put it, "troubled and changed me through its rough charm."[49] Degas, who all his life passionately experimented with various printing techniques, once exclaimed before Redon's lithographs: "What he wants to say I often do not understand ... but his blacks! oh! his blacks ... impossible to pull any of equal beauty...."[50]

Soon after their first meeting, Hennequin had brought the artist Flaubert's *Temptation of St. Anthony* which Redon discovered to be "a literary marvel and a mine for me,"[51] a mine that eventually was to inspire several series of lithographs.

Whereas there were now collectors who subscribed to Redon's lithographic publications, and writers who cultivated his friendship, a real contact with the young among the artists was not yet established since the Independents had failed to provide it. No wonder, then, that when Redon was invited by the group of Belgian avant-garde painters, *Les Vingt*,[52] to exhibit with them in 1886, he accepted "with a feeling of joy—a sweet reward."[53] But among all the participants in the Brussels show (including Monet and Renoir), it was Redon who was most savagely maligned by the critics. They particularly attacked the evocative captions with which he frequently endowed his lithographs, the very captions of whose poetic wording Mallarmé professed to be jealous. Nevertheless, Redon was to gain several extremely ardent friends and admirers in Belgium, such as the poet Verhaeren, Jules Destrée, who soon began work on a first catalogue of Redon's lithographs, and the lawyer Edmond Picard, who commissioned him to do a series of illustrations for his play, *Le juré*. The warm support which the artist unexpectedly found beyond the frontiers of France was to be a source of satisfaction.

In Paris, meanwhile, Redon was invited by Guillaumin, whom he had met at the Independents, to participate in 1886 in the eighth—and last—group show of the impressionists. Although he considered impressionism somewhat "low of ceiling," Redon joined Guillaumin and his associates, among them Pissarro, Degas, Berthe Morisot, Mary Cassatt, Gauguin, Seurat, and Signac. His drawings were hung in a hallway where, according to Huysmans, they attracted many visitors. But the struggle was far from over. This had become evident when Octave Mirbeau, staunch supporter of the impressionists and close friend of Zola, published shortly before the opening of the exhibition an article in *Le Gaulois* (where Redon had shown his drawings in 1882), bitingly attacking the artist in the name of "naturalism":

"After innumerable battles, all pacific by the way and in which only ink was spattered, everybody agrees that it is necessary for art to approach nature.... Among painters there is hardly anybody except M. Odilon Redon who resists the great naturalist current and who opposes the thing dreamed to the thing experienced, the ideal to the truth. Thus M. Redon draws for you an eye which floats, at the end of a stem, in an amorphous landscape. And the commentators assemble [precisely what the artist did not want them to do!].

Some will tell you that this eye exactly represents the eye of Conscience, others the eye of Incertitude; some will explain that this eye synthesizes a setting sun over hyperborean seas, others that it symbolizes universal sorrow, a bizarre water lily about to blossom on the black waters of invisible Acherons. A supreme exegete arrives and concludes: 'This eye at the end of a stem is simply a necktie pin.' The very essence of the ideal is that it evokes nothing but vague forms which might just as well be magic lakes as sacred elephants, extra-terrestrial flowers as well as necktie pins, unless they are nothing at all. Yet, we demand today that whatever is represented be precise, we want the figures that emanate from an artist's brain to move and think and live."[54]

Nobody shall ever know how Redon reacted to these cruel words. When they appeared, towards the end of April 1886, he was at Peyrelebade where, in May, his wife gave birth to a son. The artist's happiness knew no bounds; it was "strong and healthy and real," such as he had never experienced. It was, as he put it, like "a shock in the bowels, as if my forces, weary and worn, had gained new resilience."[55] And then tragedy struck. After a few months the infant died.

Sadness is one thing, helpless acceptance of the brutal blows of fate is another. When grief reaches a depth where it paralyzes the mind and contracts the heart, a dreadful emptiness invades the soul, a dismal lassitude cripples the will. Even the solace of creation loses its appeal. Create what and how—when the supreme creation, the origination of life itself, has been frustated by the grim reaper who formerly had been merely a symbol among symbols? When, after a long interval, Redon went back to work and conceived a series of lithographs inspired by Flaubert's *Temptation of St. Anthony* (they were not illustrations in the proper sense, though they carry as captions some sentences taken from the text), he chose to interpret the words uttered by Death:" Mine irony surpasseth all others." But the image he invented

was completely devoid of irony. Out of a sweeping spiral emerges a sinister figure in the throes of agony rather than one exuding macabre sarcasm. And when he made a series of drawings for Baudelaire's *Flowers of Evil*, there was among them one of a white tombstone in a gloomy setting. Little by little, charcoal drawings now lost some of their attraction and Redon devoted more time to lithography.

Between 1888 and 1892 Redon seems to have returned less frequently to Peyrelebade where sad memories must have oppressed him. He spent his summers

Redon: *Death*. 1889. Lithograph, $10^1/_4 \times 7^3/_4''$. The Art Institute of Chicago. The Stickney Fund

not far from Paris, at Samois on the Seine, near Mallarmé, who stayed regularly at Valvins on the opposite bank of the river. The two friends saw each other almost daily and communicated as much in the silence of their sensitivities as in the exchange of meditations or in the fraternity of enjoyment shared. Often they went rowing together in Mallarmé's small boat. The poet, anxious to see Redon gain the recognition due him, elaborated projects of exhibitions and discussed means of using his influence to further his friend's career. In July 1888 they were joined by Hennequin whom Redon had invited to Samois. Before his host's eyes Hennequin drowned there while bathing.

Death relented at last when, at the end of April 1889, a second son was born to Redon. Mallarmé's daughter became his godmother. His parents doted with zealous care on the child who developed into a normal, healthy boy. His progress filled them with untold bliss. But youth entered Redon's life not only through the appearance of his son Arï. A new generation of painters began to manifest its admiration for him and to seek his advice. He welcomed it with an open heart.

Around 1889, Emile Bernard, then barely twenty-one, asked a friend to present him to Redon in order to pay him, after several years of devoted attention, "the enthusiastic respect one feels for genius."[56] From then on, and as his friendship with the older man became closer, he never ceased to proclaim in words and writings his admiration for Redon.[57] There can be no doubt that he discussed Redon's work with Gauguin, who may have met the artist at the 1886 impressionist exhibition. He later repeatedly spoke to Cézanne of his passion and the latter wrote to Bernard: "I have already told you that I like Redon's talent a great deal and that I agree from the bottom of my heart with his feeling and admiration for Delacroix."[58] Though he failed to convince Vincent van Gogh of Redon's merits, it was Bernard who introduced Theo van Gogh's best friend

and brother-in-law, Andries Bonger, to the master. Bonger became after 1890 an avid collector of Redon's work, assembling over many years of cordial relations with the artist an outstanding group of his masterpieces. He also actively spread the renown of Redon in his native Holland. It was to Bonger that Redon dedicated his *Confidences d'artiste*, the sensitive and revealing pages in which he analyzed his evolution and his aims. In Belgium also, Redon's stature continued to increase; in 1890 he showed again as guest of *Les Vingt* and even attended the exhibition, accompanied by Mallarmé.

Through André Mellerio (who was to become his biographer), Redon met at about the same time Maurice Denis, turned twenty in 1890, one of the most subtle and erudite minds among the young painters. And little by little all of Denis' Nabis friends, Bonnard, Vuillard, Maillol, but especially Sérusier, who had infused his comrades with the synthetist gospel of Gauguin, became frequent callers with whom Redon gladly discussed problems of art, and whose progress he followed with keen interest. "Odilon Redon never actually taught," Sérusier later said, "but the artists who had the good fortune of being admitted into his intimacy always left enriched in knowledge, encouraged, and comforted."[59]

After some twenty years of friendship with Redon, the Nabis—having by then won a certain acclaim for themselves—were to pay touching tributes to their chosen mentor. "I have the greatest admiration for Redon," Bonnard stated. "What strikes me most in his work is the blending of two almost opposite features: a very pure plastic substance and a very mysterious expression. As a person he is full of kindness and understanding. Our entire generation has experienced his charm and received his advice."[60] Maurice Denis, who was to become an intimate of Redon's friend Chausson, went even further when he declared: "Redon has been one of my masters and one of the friendships of my youth. Very cultivated, musically gifted, easy of ac-

Redon: *Paul Sérusier*. 1903. Lithograph, 6³/₈ × 5¹/₄″. The Art Institute of Chicago. The Stickney Fund

cess, and kind ... he was the ideal of the Symbolist generation—he was our Mallarmé. Before Cézanne's influence made itself felt through Gauguin and Bernard, it was Redon who, with his series of lithographs and admirable charcoal drawings, determined in a spiritual sense the evolution of art around 1890. He is at the origin of all esthetic innovations or renovations, of all the revolutions of taste which we have witnessed since then ... The lesson of Redon was his incapacity to paint anything which did not represent a state of soul, which does not express some profound emotion, which does not translate an interior vision."[61]

Redon fully reciprocated the affection of these friends. He invited them to the country, drew remarkably delicate portraits of them, and once, when the by-then famous Renoir was discussed, said warmly: "Yes, Renoir does beautiful things, but the young people of today will do even better."[62]

The artist's ascendency over the new generation was publicly acknowledged when Albert Aurier, Symbolist poet and the art critic who had written the first significant articles on van Gogh and on Gauguin, hailed Redon among "the bearers of the glad tidings which the young like to invoke," as one of the uncontested initiators of the new idealistic art movement.[63]

Eventually even Gauguin was drawn towards Redon, one of the very few contemporaries of whom he spoke with unrestricted respect. Having left Brittany in the fall of 1890 for Paris where he mingled with the Symbolist poets, Gauguin saw a great deal of Redon and exchanged a small piece of pottery for the lithograph of Death (page 34). After reading J.-K. Huysmans' *Certains*, published in 1889, Gauguin jotted down some notes, taking issue with the writer's opinions on art. Huysmans had spoken once more of his friend Redon, this time in a chapter called *Le Monstre*, and Gauguin objected:

"I do not see how Redon makes monsters," Gauguin wrote. "Those are imaginary beings. He is a dreamer, a visionary. ... Nature has mysterious infinities, a power of imagination; it manifests them by always varying its products. The artist himself is one of nature's means and, to me, Redon is one of those chosen for the continuance of its creations. His dreams become reality through the probability he gives them. All his plants, his embryonic beings are essentially human, have lived with us; they certainly have their share of suffering. ... Redon speaks with his crayon; is it matter that he is after with that inner eye? In all his work I see only the language of the heart, very human and not at all monstrous. What does the means of expression matter! Impulsive movement of the heart."[64]

Gauguin continued contrasting Redon with Moreau, of whose works he knew only the theatrical compositions since Moreau never showed the bolder paintings in which he abandoned to an astonishing degree all attempts at realistic representation. In any case, Gauguin became the first to oppose the general tendency of always linking Moreau and Redon:

"Huysmans writes of Gustave Moreau with very great esteem. Well, we also have esteem for him—but to what extent? Here is a mind which is essentially not literary yet which desires to be so. Thus Moreau only speaks a language which has already been used by men of letters; it is in a certain way the illustration of ancient tales. His impulsive movement is very far from the heart and he loves the richness of material wealth. He puts it everywhere. Of every human being he makes a piece of jewelry covered with jewelry.... In fact, Moreau is an excellent chaser."[64]

There can be no doubt that in debates with his Symbolist friends Gauguin expressed similar views. If he did not induce their admiration for Redon—whom they already appreciated—at least he may have helped them to better understand him and may have contributed to their replacing a purely literary approach by one more conscious of Redon's artistic and plastic qualities. In this way Gauguin possibly played a valuable role in the art appreciation of the Symbolist writers.

An odd thing happened when Gauguin, recommended by none other than Mallarmé, went to see Octave Mirbeau in order to solicit an article to draw attention to the auction which he was preparing prior to his departure for the tropics. Mirbeau who, a few years before, had so bitterly attacked Redon in the name of "naturalism," now wrote on Gauguin in terms which might have been suitable for an essay on Redon, describing Gauguin's work as "strangely cerebral and moving, still uneven, but poignant and superb even in its irregularities. A sad work, for in order to understand it, to feel the impact of it, one must have known sorrow and the irony of sorrow, which is the threshold to mystery. Sometimes it rises to the height of a mystical act of faith; sometimes it shrinks and grimaces in the frightening gloom of doubt. And always it emits the bitter and violent aroma of the poisons of the flesh. There is in his work a disquieting and savory mixture of barbaric splendor, of Catholic liturgy, of Hindu reverie, of Gothic imagery, of obscure and subtle symbolism; there are harsh realities and frantic flights into poetry, through which M. Gauguin creates an absolutely personal and altogether new art—the art of a painter and a poet, of an apostle and a demon, an art which inspires anguish."[65]

Though Redon was doubtless happy to see his friend obtain some much needed publicity, he must also have been dismayed by Mirbeau's change of attitude. Was it the hope that the writer would now be able to understand him better, was it Mallarmé's intervention which prompted Redon to send Mirbeau his album on the Temptation of St. Anthony? Whatever the reason, the moving letter he received amply compensated for the previous offense.

"I have received the series of lithographs for St. Anthony," Mirbeau wrote. "I knew them already. But what joy to have them from you! And what a surprise, too, for I did not think that you could like me sufficiently to do me this great honor. These pages for The Temptation, so uniquely yours, are among the most admirable and most alarming of yours I know. I should like to talk to you about them, to tell you all that I feel before these beautiful, so hermitically beautiful imaginings. But what can one say in a letter? Also, it seems to me that there are in me things that can express themselves only face to face with you....

"Let me say, Monsieur, that at first I rejected you, not in your *craftsmanship*, which I have always considered superb, but in your philosophy. Yet today there is no artist for whom I have the passion I have for you, because there is none who has opened to my mind such distant, such luminous, such sorrowful horizons on Mystery, that is to say on the only true life. And I believe, Monsieur—and I know of no higher praise I can give you—I believe that I understood and loved you from the day I learned to suffer."[66]

Although Redon was greatly distressed when his friend Clavaud died in December 1890 (the following year he dedicated a new series of lithographs, *Songes*, to his memory), the sadness to which he was prone slowly disappeared from his work. And as a symbol of peace and joy, he now turned to color which thus replaced the black shadows of sorrowful years. He began using pastel, which offered the same powdery substance propitious to supple modeling as charcoal, and produced the same velvety effects. At first Redon merely enhanced some of his previous charcoal drawings with accents of color, but soon he began to use pastel for its own sake, relishing the delicate and radiant harmonies he was able to produce.

When a young Danish artist came to see Redon in 1892, he was surprised not only at the great number of charcoal drawings he was shown (which proved to him that the master "could not yet boast of a large, demanding public"), but noticed a few drawings heightened with colors, "strange and haunting colors of the Gustave Moreau type [?], powerful, massive. . . . "Redon's visitor also remarked that the artist "looked somewhat needy, but not impoverished; his surroundings were nevertheless quite humble, a tiny apartment on a fourth floor in a remote, dingy street. I believe there were only three little rooms for him, his wife, and a son; his studio was so small that there was hardly space for a decent easel."[67]

His modest circumstances, however, did not prevent Redon's mother from asking him for support, and apparently suggesting ways for him to raise money. The artist was outraged, not so much because there were so few bonds between them—bonds which the discussions over Peyrelebade had turned into a relationship dominated by lawyers and bailiffs—but because his two brothers who sided with their mother were much better off financially, besides being bachelors and in steady government employ. He therefore pointed out to her:

"Please consider that my position is altogether uncertain, since I only produce art. I am not a civil servant and not on the government's payroll. As to increasing my revenues by giving lessons, I can't do this because I do not believe in the teaching of art. I am creating mine according to my own laws. Anything that I was taught conflicted with my nature and was nefarious. Instructing others, I would fear becoming nefarious myself.

"And I do not see the possibility of raising money in selling pieces of my furniture, as you seem to imply. It is too plain. I have accomplished my work on a three francs easel. The eight or nine thousand lithographs which I have published with great difficulties, I have made on a deal table worth four francs fifty centimes. I can assure you that true art does not enrich the one who makes it. You can believe me. I've had the experience. I possess nothing. There are but a few francs in my wallet."[68]

When, after years of uncertainty, torment, and silent struggle, Peyrelebade was finally sold in 1897, Redon felt relieved that a solution had been reached at last, though he was heartbroken over it. His brothers had offered over a quarter million francs to repurchase the domain from their creditors, but had failed. Actually, even the price obtained did not cover the mortgages, so that the family was still left with debts which the artist shared. For a few years, the new owner allowed Redon to return and spend his summers on the estate. It was from Peyrelebade that he wrote in August 1898 to a friend:

"In reality this big transaction, through which was sold hardly anything but the imprint of memories, merely consisted in affixing a little bit of ink to some papers. The result, however, is an immense and unimaginable relief which shows me how great a portion of reason I uselessly expended here. It is impossible that this will not, henceforth, have its repercussions on my work. . . . It is said that what gives man his greatest happiness is the contemplation of things that do not belong to him, such as the sea, the mountains, or a beautiful act of heroism. That is evident; but happiness and the creation of art do not come from the same still. . . . The artist participates in the objects which he appropriates and does not dwell in abstraction as much as one might think—I feel completely uprooted."[69]

Though the loss of Peyrelebade was cruel, the artist's son was to say that it was "a sort of deliverance: the rupture with an entire past of distress and anguish, the end of a nightmare, of a bewitching spell. Now, with liberty regained, the door was opened widely to life and to light. A new and beautiful existence began. After so many dark days it was the dawn of a long and happy period."[70]

This new and bright phase had been forecast since the early nineties by the introduction of color into Redon's work and by various events which ever more forcefully drew him out of his isolation. In 1894 he held his first important one-man show of over 130 drawings, paintings, pastels, lithographs, and etchings. It did not take place on make-shift premises, like his previous small exhibitions, but in the large galleries of Durand-Ruel. The catalogue introduction was written by Mellerio and among the lenders were Mallarmé, Huysmans, Edmond Picard, Hennequin's widow, the critic Roger Marx, Ernest Chausson (who owned the painting *Virgin of Dawn*), Ambroise Vollard, a young dealer recently established in Paris, and a still little-known friend of Mallarmé and Maurice Denis, André Gide. The press comments were favorable, although Redon deplored that "every pen tries to link me to its creed. They are mistaken in supposing that I have any specific purpose. I only create art."[1]

It was after this succesful exhibition that Redon, now in his middle fifties, wrote to his friend Picard in Brussels: "I feel the coming of the hour where time doubles its price, the instant where the artist knows himself and no longer goes astray. Master of my means —in a small domain—I experience more than ever the pleasures which work procures. With pastel I have recovered the hope of giving my dreams greater plasticity, if possible. Colors contain a joy which relaxes me; besides, they sway me toward something different and new. Yet I could not speak to you of my projects; one doesn't know the art of tomorrow."[1]

The discovery or rediscovery of color (used sparingly in the portrait of his wife painted in 1882, page 55) not only transformed the mood of Redon's works, it also completely changed—as it had to—the range of his subject matter. Somber visions were succeeded by happier ones, but visions his subjects remained. Seldom was the artist attracted by the direct representation of his observations, except when he did portraits, a few still lifes, or had models pose for nudes (an infrequent occurrence, page 74). As in the past, reality observed usually led to flights into fantasy. When Redon once lived near the premises of a horse-dealer, for instance, he conceived a series of works representing Pegasus or Apollo's chariot.[71] His inspiration still needed few props, just as the narrowness of his studio could not limit the vast regions which his imagination visited. If Redon now often turned to mythology or the Bible for subjects, he did so mostly to provide his compositions with some plausible theme rather than to illustrate any specific episodes of Olympian sagas or of the Scriptures. This approach eliminated the necessity for explanatory details or attributes while permitting the artist to place imaginary figures in imaginary settings for the sake of evocative combinations. Even religious subjects were pretexts for images throbbing with fervor and compassion (page 102), although Redon remained aloof from all orthodox devotion. When, toward 1895, Huysmans embraced Catholicism, the artist respected his decision; but when the writer tried to convert his friend, Redon disengaged himself, determined to remain free in his own beliefs.

Redon's subjects were only simple incidents in the general arrangement of colors and forms. No doubt his horror of empty, white surfaces continued to prompt him to start each pastel by scrawling chalk colors on his sheet to "bring it to life" and to invoke inspiration. It seemed immaterial whether a subtle expanse of clouds was enhanced by a cavalcade of horses and transformed into a representation of Phaeton (pages 78, 79), whether some mysterious cliffs and swelling waves were complemented by small figures which turned the scene into Perseus delivering Andromeda, or whether almost abstract forms floating on a neutral background were adorned with vague floral ornaments and thus became purely invented animals of the sea (page 76). All that mattered was that colors, space, design, texture, composition were organized according to the dictate of Redon's creative will.

That this will continued to obey his inspiration relieved the artist of the necessity of using color realistically; on the contrary, it induced him to the greatest freedom, of which he took full advantage. No wonder then that André Masson has called Redon "perhaps the first really free colorist," crediting him with the demonstration of "the endless possibilities of lyrical chromatics." According to Masson, Redon invented "color as metamorphosis," and used his "tight-rope hues to the limits of the possible."[72] Indeed, the figures and the faces, the aquatic fauna and the butterflies, but above all the unending succession of fabulous blossoms which Redon brought into existence make no pretense at representing natural truth. They are, more often than not, prolongations of dreams, happy dreams vying with the splendors of the rainbow.

In the late nineties, Redon took up his brushes again, not to put them down anymore. He now used both pastel and oils to explore the realm of color. In his oil paintings he found new attraction in surface texture, from thin washes to heavy impasto, often combining them on the same canvas (page 83).

In the same way in which his first lithographs had been transpositions of earlier drawings, some of his paintings were translations of subjects previously treated in lithographs. The ironic Death, whose image continued to haunt the artist, reappeared, surging through intense tonalities (page 75). Certain feminine profiles were repeated again and again, surrounded by delicate ornaments and tints (pages 71–73). Even the animals of the sea echoed similar creatures represented in lithographs. Occasionally the artist also took up works abandoned or completed years before: some figures added to an early landscape of Peyrelebade changed it into The Rest on the Flight into Egypt; a vase of flowers, turned sidewise, became an Ophelia through the addition of a girl's profile (page 80); an abstractly patterned surface with superb red accents was transposed into a celestial expanse by the imposition of a winged effigy (page 65).

In 1896 Redon published two more albums of lithographs, at the same time experimenting with color lithography. One of the last series he then undertook was destined to illustrate Mallarmé's *Coup de dés* ... which the poet came to read to the artist in 1897. The publication, which Vollard planned to issue, would at last have united the names of the two friends on the same title page. Redon set to work with enthusiasm and told Mallarmé that he planned to draw "blond and pale" images that would harmonize with the typography selected by Vollard.[73] But the project came to naught when Mallarmé died in September 1898. Redon wept upon learning the news. Less than a year later, Ernest Chausson perished in an accident.

In 1902 Redon painted for Chausson's widow a series of decorative panels for a small room. He also executed various other decorations and screens for friends, among them Bonger and Fayet, a patron of Gauguin.

Redon: *Decorative panel.* (1902). Oil and gouache on canvas, 8′ 4⁵/₈″ × 6′ 1³/₄″. Private collection, Charlotte, Vermont. (Originally executed for Mme Ernest Chausson)

Gauguin himself, after his return from Tahiti, had persuaded an English artist to purchase a series of Redon's lithographs, but an exhibition which was held in 1895 in London did not prove particularly successful. In an article Gauguin once more spoke admiringly of Redon, calling him "this extraordinary artist whom people obstinately refuse to understand. Will they ever do him justice? Yes, when all his imitators have been placed on pedestals."[74] Actually Redon had no imitators and slowly began to win wider recognition.

The year 1899 witnessed a kind of apotheosis when several groups of young artists decided to "concentrate the various aspects of contemporary tendencies" in a large exhibition held at Durand-Ruel's. The Nabis were represented by Bonnard, Denis, Sérusier, Vuillard, and others. Among the neo-impressionists who participated were Cross, Signac, and van Rysselberghe. A group who called themselves the "colorists" delegated Albert André, d'Espagnat, Valtat, etc.; and the Rosicrucians appeared with Bernard, Filiger, La Rochefoucauld. The only artist listed by himself and, as it were, the dean of the exhibitors, was Redon. He was the lonely master belonging to no group, revered by all for the high and pure example he set.[75]

A little later Denis decided to honor Cézanne with a large composition in which, grouped around a still life by the artist that had belonged to Gauguin, he assembled his friends: Vuillard, Sérusier, Mellerio, Bonnard, Vollard, and several others. Since he had never met Cézanne, he could not include him. Instead he put Redon at the extreme left of his large canvas, near the easel with the still life, in front of which stands Sérusier, his hands stretched toward Redon. Denis' *Hommage à Cézanne,* exhibited at the Salon of 1901 (and purchased by Gide[76]), thus became at the same time an homage to Redon. He accepted it with unpretentious pride.

In 1904, the *Salon d'Automne* was founded and Redon became one of its charter members, together with Roger Marx, Huysmans, and several pupils of Moreau, among them Rouault. He subsequently used his influence to organize a Bresdin retrospective for which he wrote the foreword. At the first annual of the new Salon, an entire room was devoted to Redon himself, at last revealing to the general public the full impact of his transformation into a master of the palette. There was also a succession of one-man shows. In 1898

41

Vollard had exhibited a group of drawings and pastels, and since then had manifested an active interest in Redon, whom he supported effectively. In 1900 Durand-Ruel again showed his work, in 1901 it was once more Vollard's turn, and in 1903 and 1906 again that of Durand-Ruel.

The renown that came after he had passed sixty provided Redon with a certain well-being, though he by no means exploited the favorable current. He was, in the words of his son, "embarrassed to be obliged, whenever he sold a painting, to set a price for it, and he almost apologized to his collectors, for fear that the amount stipulated might appear too high."[77] This situation was further complicated by the fact that practically all the collectors who directly approached the artist soon became personal friends, irresistibly attracted by his saintly goodness, supreme intelligence, and high culture; commercial transactions proved even more delicate under the circumstances.

When, in 1905, Redon looked for new and larger quarters, he was satisfied, as before, to use a well-lit room for his work rather than to search for a regular studio. He moved into a spacious apartment (which his son still occupies) on the quiet, bourgeois Avenue de Wagram. Indeed, he contented himself with providing for the modest needs of his little family without trying to amass any fortune or to change his mode of existence. He therefore could not call on any reserves when the sorry affairs of Peyrelebade, after festering for so many years, claimed his participation in settling old debts. He decided to solve the problem by giving up the greater part of his production and holding a public auction. In the summer of 1906 he wrote to his friend Bonger: "I wish to come out of this with dignity and honor. The sale will produce what it can; after that my heart shall be soothed for having done all that was possible in the face of destiny. Never will an action have intermingled more closely the life of the man with that of the artist."[78]

The auction, comprising fifty-three works, took place on March 11, 1907. Although it attracted a good deal of attention and led to a series of commissions for portraits and decorative panels, the prices obtained were low, so low that Redon himself had to buy back half of the items. But at last the obsession of Peyrelebade was liquidated once and for all. That very year Redon's brother Ernest died, whom he had not seen for about a decade, followed in 1908 by their mother.

Since before 1900 Redon had ceased to sojourn on the former family estate. Instead he rented a villa every summer in Saint-Georges-de-Didonne, a small seaside resort near Royan, north of Bordeaux, on the wide estuary of the Gironde. Redon loved the sea and the frequent visits from painters, poets, writers, and collectors. Vuillard came with his mother; Gide and Francis Jammes dropped in, Arthur Fontaine and Gustave Fayet peacefully competed in the purchase of paintings or pastels, commissioned portraits or decorations. The artist attached himself particularly to a new collector and friend, Gabriel Frizeau, who came from Bordeaux and became its first citizen to assemble a group of Redon's work. Yet the animation of these pleasant summers, the tennis he played assiduously, did not prevent Redon from painting, particularly on rainy days. At the end of each season his intimates were surprised to discover how productive he had been. "The walls of his studio were covered with pastels and paintings of flowers; the large, whitewashed room had become a real greenhouse with luxuriant vegetation."[79]

Redon was older than his companions but kept young in spirit and body. He acted as if he belonged to their generation and was embarrassed when somebody approached him with deference.[80] But how they venerated him, how they vied with each other to show him, not the respect he disliked, but genuine affection and love! The youth and enthusiasm of his friends enchanted Redon but also shone in his work, shone so brightly that the young were unendingly seized with admiration for the old man. On the occasion of one of his exhibitions at Durand-Ruel's, Denis marvelled at Redon's "flowers, portraits, and compositions of a freshness, a brilliance, and—to say it with one word—a youthfulness which surprise." At the same time Denis noticed that the master's venture into the field of decoration had led him to almost abstract designs, relying solely on color (although his palette was much more subdued in his panels than in his canvases). "He has conceived this ornamental art," commented Denis, "detached from any idea of form, of drawing, of plastic silhouettes. He has created it through contrasts and analogies of colors and tints: to render it expressive he has contented himself to combine thousands of radiant touches, without disturbing them by a gesture, a single human gesture."[81]

One of Gustave Moreau's most prominent pupils, Henri Matisse, became an admirer of Redon, in spite of the fact that Moreau had condescendingly said: "M. Redon is sincere and certainly shows a development of the intellect that is by no means banal.... But, after all, what sad results!"[82] Although in his fauve period he had reached a chromatic intensity and freedom which made him the leader of the next generation, Matisse felt greatly attracted by Redon's work, which, as he put it, "I studied with great interest—the purity and ardor of his tones pleased me."[83] Matisse not only purchased several pastels for his father and for himself, he also introduced the Russian collector Shchukin to Redon, who at his urging bought several important works from the artist.[84]

In 1912, the periodical *La Vie* published an *Hommage à Redon* with eloquent tributes from all his friends, most of them younger painters. When Kees van Dongen, one of Matisse's fellow fauves, was asked for his opinion, he simplified matters by retorting: "What do I admire in Redon's work? Everything, I admire everything he does."[85]

By that time most of Redon's great contemporaries and even some of their young successors were gone: Gauguin, Pissarro, Cézanne had died, and before them, van Gogh, Seurat, and Lautrec. Renoir lived in the South confined to a wheelchair (Redon, who was one year older than he, had visited him in 1901); Monet, in Giverny, only saw a few old friends; Degas was irascible and avoided new acquaintances. But Redon's door remained always open. The remarkable and probably unique result was that his work was being propagated mostly by fellow artists, such as Bernard, the Nabis, or Matisse. It was through a young American painter, Walter Pach, who visited Redon around 1910, that he was introduced to the United States.

As one of the organizers of the 1913 Armory Show, Pach saw to it that Redon received a particularly large representation. In fact, no other artist exhibited as many works. Matisse had fifteen, van Gogh fourteen, Gauguin twelve, Cézanne, the douanier Rousseau, and Picasso eight each, Monet, Pissarro, and Renoir four each, Degas three, and Lautrec two; Redon, however, was shown in a room with no fewer than thirty-eight paintings, pastels (and probably also drawings), twenty-nine lithographs, and seven etchings.[86] Next to Marcel Duchamp, all of whose nine paintings found purchasers, Redon sold in larger quantity than any other exhibitor. Among the buyers were John Quinn, who soon formed a representative collection of Redon's works,[87] and Lillie P. Bliss, who acquired *Roger and Angelica* as well as *Silence* (later bequeathed to the Museum of Modern Art in New York, pages 85, 93). Even those who were not prepared for the unconventional art presented by the Armory show, made an exception of Redon. Former President Theodore Roosevelt recognized the importance of the event, saying that he was "grateful to those who arranged this exhibition," although he found little to like; among the few things that attracted him were "Redon's marvelous color pieces ..."[88]

Marcel Duchamp, who emerged from the show as

one of the most talked-about and most controversial leaders of contemporary art, replied, when asked whether or not he and his colleagues derived from Cézanne: "I am sure that most of my friends would say so and I know that he is a great man. Nevertheless, if I am to tell what my own point of departure has been, I should say that it was the art of Odilon Redon."[89] And Redon himself commented on his most recent admirers: "They are a bit terrifying with some of their theories and in the lengths they are going, but no matter: when they say I have a share in their ideas, it gives me pleasure."[90]

With great serenity Redon advanced in years. He began to accept invitations, went to the theater, to the opera, and never missed a presentation of the Ballets Russes. Yet when Diaghilev asked him to design the scenery for Mallarmé's *L'Après-midi d'un faune*, he refused because of the large scale of the work to be done. Music remained his favorite distraction, particularly that of Schumann, Chopin, Gluck, Berlioz, and Beethoven. "They represent to me," he said, "the five luminous and vivifying points of a mystic star which has sustained me lightly throughout life, making me forget its rigors. Oh! that beautiful art. It is more powerful than the one I exercise."[91] (Certain Redon drawings bear annotations of musical themes in their margins.)

The only significant change which occurred late in Redon's life was the inheritance in 1910 of a comfortable house in the country not far from Paris, bequeathed to Madame Redon by her sister. He went to live there each year as soon as the days grew longer. Madame Redon planted flowers of all varieties in their garden and arranged them for him in different vases. He represented them in innumerable still lifes which he painted in a small pavilion that was shaded by large trees and had a big window overlooking the valley of the Bièvre. Most of his bouquets no longer represented imaginary blossoms but followed faithfully the colors, shapes, and textures of nature (pages 86, 92). Yet he did not renounce occasional escapes into fantasy, also working on several large canvases of ethereal nudes, Venuses, Pandoras, or Andromedas (pages 88–89), which offered him an opportunity to combine the graceful lines of slender bodies with such favorite attributes as shells or flowers.

At about the same time Redon discovered yet another medium, watercolor, which he now used frequently to represent, on white pages which enhance the delicacy of their hues, imaginary or real blossoms, butterflies, fish (page 90), all the quiet marvels of nature he never ceased to observe and admire.

"The painter who has found his technique," the aging Redon noted in his diary, "does not interest me. He rises every morning without passion and, calmly and peacefully, pursues the work begun the day before. I suspect him of a certain boredom, like that of a virtuous laborer who continues his task without the unforeseen flash of a happy minute. He does not experience the sacred torment whose source is in the unconscious and the unknown; he does not expect anything from that which will be. I love that which has never been."[92]

It was this ideal of a continuously fresh approach, of a constantly renewed enthusiasm, which endowed Redon's last flower paintings, despite their naturalistic representation, with a certain dreamlike quality. The subtlety of their colors, the harmony of their arrangements, the mastery of their execution give them an undefinable and restrained power, and a timeless glory.

Redon's last years were suddenly and brutally overshadowed by the war. Arï was drafted immediately and soon was roaming the skies in a monster much more real and more dangerous than any of those his father ever imagined. News from his son provided the only bright moments in seemingly endless months of darkness.

"Without the present scourge," he wrote to Arï, "your old friend would have ascended straight to se-

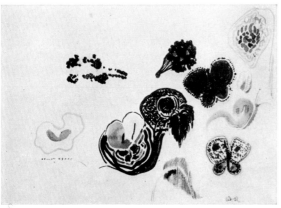

renity. With a son in the war, it is the extreme, the immeasurable ordeal for mind and heart."[93] Redon became restless and aimless, retired to Royan, to Bordeaux, visited for a last time Peyrelebade, returned to his country place, spent some winter months in Cannes, lived only from one of Arï's letters to the next. As his father had before him, the son considered war "a violent and interesting sport," yet the artist only thought of the daily perils to which Arï was exposed. Every day to him was a day closer to the end of the conflagration, but this end was nowhere in sight. Art seemed "far away," although he made an effort to continue his work, for the sake of his son. When, during the battle of Verdun, all mail was suspended, he lived in constant fear of a disaster. He fell ill but recovered through sheer power of will, because, as he wrote to Arï, "I would have been humiliated should you have found me prostrated; I did everything I could to avoid this."[94] His health failed, however, and after a relapse he died on July 6, 1916.[95] His son, recalled from the front, arrived too late.

In better days, Redon had once written: "The artist . . . will always be a special emissary—isolated, alone— with an innate sense for the organization of matter."[1] But Redon is no longer isolated, alone. He has taken his place among the privileged number of those whom posterity has elected because their gift to humanity illuminates the sky above our present and our future.

JOHN REWALD

above: Redon: *Butterflies and Sea Horses.* (1910–14). Watercolor, 6 × 9¹/₈″. Private collection, New York

left: Redon: *Butterflies and Plants.* (1910–14). Watercolor, 6³/₄ × 9¹/₄″. Musée du Petit Palais, Paris. Donation Jacques Zoubaloff

References to the posthumous publication of Redon's autobiographical essays, diary entries, notes, articles, etc. under the title: *A soi-même* (1867–1915), Paris, 1922, are abbreviated as ASM. However, this volume does not contain all of the artist's writings; some have been quoted from other sources, as indicated.

The volume of *Lettres d'Odilon Redon*, published in 1923, is by no means complete, so that many letters are here quoted from other publications. A certain number of letters are still unpublished.

Neither Redon's diary nor his correspondence have as yet appeared in English. Many excerpts from them are here translated for the first time. Unfortunately, limitations of space have prevented more extensive quotation of these texts which rank among the most beautiful writings of modern artists. Their exquisite style could only be approximated in the English versions.

1 Redon: Letter to E. Picard (June 15, 1894), written in reply to questions asked by Redon's friend who was preparing a lecture on the artist. This letter was first published in Dutch in *Nieuwe Rotterdamsche Courant*, July 4, 1894, and subsequently in the original French in *L'Art Moderne*, periodical of the Belgian association *Les Vingt*, Aug. 25, 1894. It appeared under the title "Confidences d'artiste," a title Redon used again for another, longer autobiographical text of 1909, dedicated to A. Bonger and reprinted *in* ASM, p. 11–30. In spite of their titles, the two texts are not at all identical. While excerpts from the Letter to Picard have appeared *in* A. Mellerio: Odilon Redon, Paris, 1913, p. 80–83, all quotations here are based on its publication in *L'Art Moderne*.

2 J. Doin: Odilon Redon, *Mercure de France*, July 1, 1914, p. 5–22. This excellent article was written after thorough consultations with the artist who read (and revised) it before publication; thus it complements authoritatively his own writings.

3 Redon: Confidences d'artiste (May 1909), reprinted *in* ASM, p. 11–30. See note 1.

4 Redon: Notes (1910), ASM, p. 112.

5 Redon: Letter to Dr. Sabouraud (1914), *in* Lettres d'Odilon Redon, Paris–Brussels, 1923, p. 117.

6 Redon: Delacroix (1878), *in* ASM, p. 162–174.

7 Baudelaire's Les phares, poem *in* Les fleurs du mal, first published in 1857, contains glorifications of Rembrandt, "triste hôpital rempli de murmures," of Goya, "cauchemar plein de choses inconnues," of Delacroix, "lac de sang hanté de mauvais anges."

8 Ernest Redon: Letter to his brother Odilon (1861), *in* Lettres à Odilon Redon, Paris, 1960, p. 35.

9 Redon: Letter to A. Bonger (1896); see R. Bacou: Odilon Redon, Geneva, 1956, v. I, p. 34–35.

10 Redon: Rodolphe Bresdin, preface for the retrospective, Salon d'Automne, Paris, 1908 (not included in ASM). For a complete translation see pp. 162–164.

11 Redon: Notes for a lecture delivered in Holland (Jan. 1913), *in* ASM, p. 118–133; for excerpts see pp. 164–167.

12 Redon: Note (1868), *ibid.*, p. 35–36.

13 Redon: unpublished note, courtesy M. Arï Redon, Paris.

14 Redon: Notes (1867–68), *in* ASM, p. 34–35.

15 Redon: Letter to A. Bonger (1894); see J. B. Oosting: Odilon Redon, *Maandblad voor Beeldende Kunsten*, July 1949, p. 176.

16 See J. Doin, *op. cit.*, p. 9.

17 Redon: Letter to A. Bonger (1909); see S. Sandström: Le monde imaginaire d'Odilon Redon, Lund, 1955, p. 208, note 1.

18 Baudelaire: Salon de 1859, *in* Baudelaire: Variétés critiques, Paris, 1924, v. II, p. 24.

19 Baudelaire: Salon de 1846, *in* Curiosités esthétiques; Baudelaire: Oeuvres complètes, Paris, 1923, p. 196.

20 Redon: Salon de 1868, I – Le paysage: MM. Chintreuil, Corot et Daubigny, *La Gironde*, May 19, 1868.

21 Redon: Salon de 1868, II – MM. Courbet, Manet, Pissarro, Jongkind, Monet, *La Gironde*, June 9, 1868.

22 Redon: Salon de 1868, III – MM. Fromentin, Ribot, Roybet, *La Gironde*, July 1, 1868. (These three Salon reviews – notes 20–22 – are not included in ASM.)

23 See S. Gorin's letter to Redon (1870), *in* Lettres à Odilon Redon, *op. cit.*, p. 62.

24 See the two letters from Carré to Redon (1870), *ibid.*, p. 58–60.

25 Ernest Redon: Letter to his brother Odilon (Dec. 31, 1870),

ibid., p. 44–45. The letter continues: "But how you must have suffered, my poor brother. That night before the battle, what anguish, and how many grievous sighs must have oppressed you in thinking of all the loved ones, so far and so unaware of the awful hours which lay ahead of you. Mother cried upon reading your letter, and so did father. . . . Fortunately, there are states of grace; you speak of temerity and enthusiasm in face of the enemy, you, the delicate and so highly impressionable being. Yet also what paradise, that soft night in Tours after the combat. Now you have experienced the two most terrible extremes of suffering and happiness. Your artist's soul will know how to benefit from this. . . . But having done your share, you may well, it seems to me, try to obtain a less dangerous assignment, conforming more to your disposition and nature. Those forced marches must have ruined you; I don't understand why you did not become ill."

26 Redon: Notes (1872), *in* ASM, p. 44.

27 Redon: Notes for a lecture delivered in Holland (1913), *ibid.*

28 See Arï Redon: Preface to Lettres à Odilon Redon, *op. cit.*, p. 11.

29 Redon himself has said on this subject: "No, one should not bind one's art to political convictions or to moral issues. To the contrary, art should provide the philosopher, the thinker, the scientist, and maybe even the theosophist— who knows?—with material for speculation and love." Notes (1909), *in* ASM, p. 108–109.

30 Redon: Letter to A. Mellerio (Aug. 1898), *in* Lettres d'Odilon Redon, *op. cit.*, p. 33–34.

31 On the sources of Redon's inspiration see S. Sandström, *op. cit.*

32 Redon: Letter to Mellerio (Oct. 1898), *in* Lettres d'Odilon Redon, *op. cit.*, p. 37.

33 Redon: Réflexions sur une exposition des impressionnistes (1880), *in* ASM, p. 155–156.

34 Redon: Notes taken on a trip to Holland (1878), *ibid.*, p. 72–81.

35 Redon: Letter to E. Hennequin (Aug. 1882); see Auriant: Des lettres inédites d'Odilon Redon, *Beaux-Arts*, June 7, 1935.

36 J.-K. Huysmans: Le Salon officiel de 1881, footnote; reprinted *in* Huysmans: L'art moderne, Paris, 1883, p. 215.

37 Huysmans, article of 1882, reprinted *ibid.*, appendix, p. 298–300.

38 Huysmans: Letter to Redon (Feb. 12, 1882), *in* Lettres à Odilon Redon, *op. cit.*, p. 98.

39 On this subject see Rewald: Post-Impressionism – From van Gogh to Gauguin, New York, 1956, chapter III: Symbolists and Anarchists from Mallarmé to Redon.

40 H. de Régnier, article in *Ecrits pour l'Art*, June 7, 1887.

41 Huysmans: A Rebours, Paris, 1884; English translation: Against the Grain.

42 E. Hennequin: Odilon Redon, *Revue littéraire et artistique*, March 4, 1882.

43 Redon: Letter to Hennequin (March 5, 1882); see Auriant, *op. cit.*

44 On the founding of the *Société des Artistes Indépendants* see Rewald: The History of Impressionism, New York, 1961 (revised, enlarged edition), chapter XIII.

45 Redon: Diary entry (1888), *in* ASM, p. 89.

46 Signac: Diary entry (Feb. 2, 1899); see Extraits du journal inédit de Paul Signac, III, *Gazette des Beaux-Arts*, July–Aug. 1953.

47 J. Moréas: Le Symbolisme, *Figaro Littéraire*, Sept. 18, 1886.

48 See Mallarmé's letter to Redon (Feb. 2, 1885), *in* Lettres à Odilon Redon, *op. cit.*, p. 132–133.

49 Redon: Letter to Mellerio (July 1898), *in* Lettres d'Odilon Redon, *op. cit.*, p. 31.

50 Degas, quoted by T. Natanson: Peints à leur tour, Paris, 1948, p. 48.

51 Redon: Letter to Hennequin (March 31, 1882); see Auriant, *op. cit.*

52 On *Les Vingt* see M.-O. Maus: Trente années de lutte pour l'art, 1884–1914, Brussels, 1926, and Rewald: Post-Impressionism, *op. cit.*, notably p. 101.

53 Redon: Letter to O. Maus (1885), *in* M.-O. Maus, *op. cit.*, p. 44.

54 O. Mirbeau: L'Art et la Nature, *Le Gaulois*, April 26, 1886.

55 Redon: Diary entry (May 6, 1887), written almost a year after the birth of the child, born Peyrelebade, May 11, 1886, died Paris, Nov. 27, 1886; *in* ASM, p. 86–89.

56 E. Bernard: Odilon Redon, *in* Recueil de Lettres à Emile Bernard, Tonnerre, 1925–27, p. 103 (contains 13 letters by Redon to Bernard).

57 See Rewald: Quelques notes et documents sur Odilon Redon, *Gazette des Beaux-Arts*, Nov. 1956.

58 Cézanne: Letter to E. Bernard (May 12, 1904), *in* Cézanne: Letters, London, 1941 (here newly translated).

59 Sérusier: "Hommage à Redon," *La Vie*, Nov. 30, 1912.

60 Bonnard: "Hommage à Redon" *ibid.*

61 Denis: "Hommage à Redon," *ibid.*

62 See H. Hahnloser-Bühler: Felix Vallotton et ses amis, Pa-

ris, 1936, p.104. On a visit Redon paid to Renoir in 1901 see his letter to Mme Gobillard (Cannes, Feb. 26, 1901) *in* Lettres d'Odilon Redon, *op. cit.*, p. 46, in which he wrote: "... I saw Renoir suffering from pain but very beautiful in his splendid pride. He was surprised by my visit and touched at the same time. He said so gently, with something in his voice that made me perceive his exquisite sensitivity.... He lives in a house with orange trees, halfway up a hill from where a superb view unfolds all the way to the Mediterranean; it is a rather austere place where, it appears to me, it is difficult for him to have guests. This I seemed to understand when—under the pretext of the rusticity of his lodgings—he invited me to meet him Monday, yesterday, in the house of friends, at Cagnes. I didn't go, being detained here. Moreover, I preferred to keep with me the deep and soft impression which I had felt when I shook his ailing and beautiful hand."

63 A. Aurier: Les Symbolistes, *Revue Encyclopédique*, April 1, 1892; reprinted *in* Aurier: Oeuvres posthumes, Paris, 1893, p.293–309.

64 Gauguin: Huysmans et Redon (c. 1890–91); see J. Loize: Un inédit de Gauguin, *Nouvelles Littéraires*, May 7, 1953.

65 Mirbeau: Paul Gauguin, *Echo de Paris*, Feb. 16, 1891; reprinted *in* Mirbeau: Des artistes, v. I, Paris, 1922, p.119–129.

66 Mirbeau: Letter to Redon, *in* Lettres à Odilon Redon, *op. cit.*, p.248–249. The undated letter is there published as having been written in 1896, date of the appearance of Redon's third album of the *Tentation de Saint-Antoine;* however, there seems to be no proof that it does not refer to the first series of lithographs, which had appeared in 1888 and which the artist could have offered to the writer in 1891, especially since Mirbeau stated that he *already knew* the work. The letter may therefore have been sent in 1891. It should be mentioned that Mirbeau did *not* reprint his attack on Redon (see note 54) in the collection of his articles: Des artistes, *op. cit.*

67 J. Rohde: Journal fra en Rejse i 1892, Copenhagen, 1955; diary entry of May 1892, p.84–86.

68 Redon: Letter to his mother (1898), quoted *in* Preface to Lettres à Odilon Redon, *op. cit.*, p.17.

69 Redon: Excerpts from a letter to an unspecified addressee (Aug. 1898), *in* ASM, p.95. Redon had even considered buying Peyrelebade himself and had asked Ernest Chausson, who was wealthy, whether he would lend him the necessary amount. The composer immediately expressed readiness to do so but told Redon that, being an artist, he should not burden himself with the financial and other responsibilities resulting from such a purchase. Redon accepted his advice. (Information courtesy M. Arï Redon.)

70 Arï Redon: Preface to Lettres à Odilon Redon, *op. cit.*, p.17.

71 See Doin, *op. cit.*, p.13.

72 A. Masson: Mystic with a Method, *Art News*, Jan. 1957. This excellent article by one of the master's of our time offers a penetrating analysis of Redon's contribution, which is so often misunderstood when he is linked with the Surrealists.

73 See Redon's letter to Mallarmé (1898), *in* H. Mondor: Vie de Mallarmé, Paris, 1941, p.786. On these illustrations see also U. Johnson: Ambroise Vollard, éditeur, New York, 1944, p.123, No.140 and Appendix XI, p.209–211.

74 Gauguin: Sous deux latitudes, *Essais d'Art Libre*, Feb.–April 1894.

75 On this exhibition see Rewald: Quelques notes et documents sur Odilon Redon, *op. cit.*, and: Extraits du journal inédit de Paul Signac, *op. cit.*, p.38–51. Also M. Denis: Journal (1884–1904), v. I, Paris, 1957, p.151.

76 See Denis: Journal, *ibid.*, p.143 and 168–170.

77 Arï Redon: Preface, *op. cit.*, p.23.

78 Redon: Letter to A. Bonger (Aug. 1906), *in* catalogue of the exhibition Odilon Redon, Orangerie des Tuileries, Paris, Oct. 1956–Jan. 1957. No.188, p.92.

79 See Arï Redon: Preface, *op. cit.*, p.19.

80 See *ibid.*, p.22.

81 Denis: Exposition Odilon Redon, *L'Occident*, April 1903; reprinted *in* Denis: Théories (1890–1910), Paris, 1912, p.132–134.

82 Moreau quoted by C. Chassé: Le mouvement symboliste dans l'art du XIXe siècle, Paris, 1947, p.32.

83 Matisse: Letter to the author, Feb. 12, 1949.

84 When Matisse could not purchase from his father's estate the works he had acquired for him, they were sold to the American collector John Quinn (see note 87). Among them was the pastel *Orpheus* now owned by the Cleveland Museum of Art.

85 Kees van Dongen: Hommage à Redon, *La Vie*, Nov. 30, 1912. For the tributes by Sérusier, Bonnard, and Denis, published in the same issue of the periodical, whose editors were Redon's old friends, Marius and Ary Leblond, see notes 59–61.

86 The catalogue of the Armory show, which was rather inaccurate and incomplete, lists Redon's works (Nos. 271–310) as follows: Géranium; Le bouquet aux feuilles rouges; Fleurs, fond rouge; Pégase sur un roc; Fécondité, étude

48

(lent by M. Marcel Kapferer); Vase de fleurs avec géranium, No. 115; Papillons, No. 121 [possibly the painting lent by the Detroit Museum of Fine Arts to the present exhibition, No. 51]; Roses sur fond vert, No. 116; Papillon[s], No. 38; Profil noir sur fond or, No. 111; Fleurs, No. 75; Phaéton, No. 114 (lent by M. Jos. Hessel); Deux têtes dans les fleurs (lent by M. Marcel Kapferer) [probably the painting shown in the present exhibition as *Two Heads Among Flowers*, ill. p. 71]; Vieillard [probably the drawing shown in the present exhibition as No. 112]; Muse sur Pégase, No. 110; Bargue [?]; Le char d'Apollon; Fleurs dans un jut [?] de grès (lent by M. Jos. Hessel); Initiation à l'étude [now in the Dallas Museum for Contemporary Art]; Fleurs, pastel (lent by M. Wilhelm Uhde); Profil mystique, pastel; Songe d'Orient, pastel; Corbeille de fleurs; Coquelicots; Barque; Vase de fleurs, bleu; Vase de fleurs, gris; Prométhée; Tête en fleurs; Le silence [purchased by Miss Lillie P. Bliss and shown here as No. 54, ill. p. 93]; Monstre et Angélique [probably the painting owned by the Art Institute of Chicago, No. 33 of this catalogue]; Deux êtres sublunaires ailés dans l'espace; Ohannès (lent by M. Artz & de Bois); Tête de femme, pastel (lent by Mme Chadbourne); Fleurs de champs dans un vase, pastel (lent by M. Marcel Kapferer); Roger et Angélique; Tête d'Orphée; Lithographies, Nos. 1–29; Eaux-fortes, Nos. 1–7; Le bateau rouge (lent by M. W. Uhde).

In the subsequent Chicago showing three paintings were omitted, probably because the new owners did not want to lend them, and one painting, *Christ* (lent by Mrs. F. R. Lillie), was added.

It is difficult to identify most works with certainty because (a) the medium is seldom given, (b) the artist often used titles like *Phaeton* or *Papillons* for different works, and (c) some titles have since been changed, for instance, *Etruscan Vase*, which according to Walter Pach was included in the show but may have been catalogued simply as one of the flower pieces.

Apparently most of the works were lent by Redon himself, since in other instances loans from dealers, such as Durand-Ruel or Vollard, are credited to them; among the owners of Redon's works who lent to the exhibition, only Jos. Hessel was a dealer.

The numbers following some of the titles do not refer to the list which Redon kept of his works when he sold them (and which helps his son with problems of dating and authentification). The meaning of these numbers is not clear.

On the exhibition see notably W. Pach: Queer Thing, Painting, New York–London, 1938, chapter XVI, The Armory Show, p. 192–203, and M. W. Brown: American Painting from the Armory Show to the Depression, Princeton, 1955.

87 The catalogue of The John Quinn Collection of Paintings, Water Colors, Drawings & Sculpture, Huntington, N. Y., 1926, lists seven paintings, four pastels and one design for a stained glass window. Among them are *Etruscan Vase* and *Pandora*, lent by the Metropolitan Museum of Art to the present exhibition. *Etruscan Vase* had subsequently been acquired by Lillie P. Bliss.

88 T. Roosevelt, article on the Armory Show in *The Outlook*, March 29, 1913.

89 Marcel Duchamp quoted by Pach, *op. cit.*, p. 163.

90 Redon quoted by Pach, *ibid.*, p. 165.

91 Redon quoted by his son *in* Arï Redon: Preface, *op. cit.*, p. 23.

92 Redon: Diary entry (1908), *in* ASM, p. 105.

93 Redon: Letter to his son Arï (1915–16), quoted *in* Arï Redon: Preface, *op. cit.*, p. 26.

94 Redon: Letter to his son Arï (May 8, 1916), *in* Lettres d'Odilon Redon, *op. cit.*, p. 142.

95 The Parisian collector Jacques Zoubaloff, aware of the precarious situation of the artist's widow whose son had returned to the front, approached Mme Redon and offered assistance. On various occasions she called upon him and he selected a number of works which he purchased, having them delivered directly to the Musée du Petit Palais as his donation. This is probably a unique case where a collector combined help to an artist's family with a public spirit of rare generosity. None of the works he thus acquired ever entered his possession.

Redon: *Roland at Roncevaux*. (c. 1865). Pen and ink, $13^3/_8 \times 10^1/_4''$. Collection Charles K. Lock, New York

Redon: *Two Figures in a Mountain Landscape*. (c. 1865).
Pen and India ink wash on bristol board, 9⁷/₈ × 6⁵/₈″.
Musée du Petit Palais, Paris. Donation Jacques Zoubaloff

Redon: *Arab Horsemen*. (c. 1865). Oil on canvas, 11¹/₂ × 10″.
Collection Mrs. Nikifora Pach, New York

Redon: *Landscape*, *Peyrelebade*. (c. 1880). Oil on cardboard, 18¹/₈ × 17³/₈″. Collection Ari Redon, Paris

Redon: *Apparition*. (1870–75?). Pencil, 7³/₄ × 7¹/₂″. Collection Mrs. Charles E. Slatkin, New York

Redon: *Near the Harbor, Brittany.* (c. 1880). Oil, $7^1/_2 \times 10^3/_4''$. Collection Mrs. Richard J. Bernhard, New York

54

Redon: *Portrait of Mme Redon*. 1882. Oil on canvas, $17^3/_4 \times 14^1/_2''$. Musée du Louvre, Paris

Redon: *Winged Head above the Waters*. (c. 1875). Charcoal, $18^{1}/_{4} \times 14^{5}/_{8}''$. The Art Institute of Chicago. The David Adler Collection

Redon: *The Weeping Spider*. (c. 1880). Charcoal, 19^1/$_2$ × 14^3/$_4$″. Collection Dr. and Mrs. B. K. Boom, Amsterdam

Redon: *Eyes in the Forest*. (1875–80). Charcoal on brown paper, 13¹/₄ × 10³/₄″. City Art Museum of St. Louis

Redon: *Germination*. (1885). Charcoal, 20¹/₂ × 15″. Collection
Henri Dorra, Philadelphia

Redon: *The Cactus Man*. (1881). Charcoal on beige paper,
18¹/₄ × 12³/₈″. Collection Ian Woodner, New York

Redon: *Figure in Armor*. (c. 1885). Charcoal, 19⁷/₈ × 15″. The Metropolitan Museum of Art, New York. The Dick Fund, 1948

Redon: *Marsh Flower*. (c. 1885). Charcoal, 16³/₄ × 14″. Collection Mr. and Mrs. H. Lawrence Herring, New York

Redon: *A Flower with a Child's Face*. (c. 1885). Charcoal, 15⁷/₈ × 13″. The Art Institute of Chicago. The David Adler Collection

Redon: *Mask of the Red Death*. (1883). Charcoal, 16$^1/_2$ × 14$^1/_8$″. New Gallery, New York

opposite: Redon: *Symbolic Head*. (1890). Oil on canvas, 21 × 15$^1/_4$″.
Collection Mr. Peter Andrews Putnam, Cleveland

Redon: *Fallen Angel*. (1890–1905). Oil on canvas, $31^7/8 \times 39^3/8''$. E. and A. Silberman Galleries, New York

opposite: Redon: *Cyclops*. (c. 1898). Oil on wood, $25^1/4 \times 20''$.
Rijksmuseum Kröller-Müller, Otterlo

Redon: *Self Portrait*. (c. 1895?). Crayon, 13³/₈ × 8⁷/₈″. Collection Dr. J. E. van der Meulen, The Hague

Redon: *Head with Flowers*. (c. 1895). Oil on canvas, $20^1/_2 \times 18^1/_2''$. Collection Mrs. Arthur Lehman, New York

Redon: *Woman with Flowers*. (1903). Pastel, 26 × 19³/₄″. Collection Mrs. H. Harris Jonas, New York

opposite : Redon: *The Doge's Wife*. (c. 1900). Oil on canvas, 25 × 14³/₄″. Paul Rosenberg & Co., New York

Redon: *Etruscan Vase*. (1900–05). Tempera on canvas, 31³/₄×23″. The Metropolitan
Museum of Art, New York. The Maria DeWitt Jessup Fund, 1951

Redon: *Two Heads among Flowers*. (c. 1905). Oil on canvas, 24 × 19³/₄″. Private collection, Cambridge, Mass.

Redon: *Head of a Woman in a Shell.* (1912). Oil on cardboard, 21³/₈ × 21¹/₄″. Collection
Dr. Hans R. Hahnloser, Bern

opposite: Redon: *Ophelia.* (1905–06). Oil on board,
22⁷/₈ × 18¹/₈″. Collection Ian Woodner, New York

Redon: *Eve*. (1904). Oil on canvas, 24 × 18¹/₈″. Collection Jacques Dubourg, Paris

opposite : Redon: *The Green Death*. (After 1905). Oil on canvas, 21⁵/₈ × 18¹/₂″. Collection Mrs. Bertram Smith, New York

Redon: *At the Bottom of the Sea.* (c. 1905). Oil on canvas, 23 × 19″. Collection Mr. and Mrs. Charles Goldman, New York

Redon: *Arï Redon*. (1897). Pastel, 17⁷/₈ × 12³/₈″. The Art Institute of Chicago. Gift of Kate L. Brewster

opposite : Redon : *The Fall of Phaeton.* (c. 1900). Oil, 28³/₄ ×
21¹/₄″. Collection Mr. and Mrs. Werner E. Josten, New York

Redon : *Phaeton.* (c. 1910). Oil on canvas, 21 × 8¹/₄″. Collection Mr. and Mrs. Sidney Simon, New City, New York

Redon: *Ophelia*. (c. 1910). Pastel, 25 × 36″. Collection Mrs. Albert D. Lasker, New York

Redon: *Still Life: Vase of Flowers*. (c. 1910). Oil on cardboard, 27 × 21″. The Art Institute of Chicago. The Mr. and Mrs. Lewis L. Coburn Memorial Collection

Redon: *Jacob Wrestling with the Angel.* (c. 1905). Oil on wood, 18¹/₂ × 16¹/₄″. Collection Mr. and Mrs. Matthew H. Futter, New York

Redon: *Apparition*. (1910). Oil on canvas, $25^7/8 \times 20''$. The Art Museum, Princeton University

Redon: *The White Butterfly*. (c. 1910). Oil on canvas, 25 × 19¹/₄″. Collection Ian Woodner, New York

opposite: Redon: *Roger and Angelica*. (c. 1910). Pastel on paper on canvas, 36¹/₂ ×
28³/₄″. The Museum of Modern Art, New York. The Lillie P. Bliss Collection

Redon: *Flowers in a Green Vase*. (c. 1910). Oil on canvas, 21¹/₂ × 29¹/₄″. Collection The Honorable and Mrs. John Hay Whitney, New York

opposite: Redon: *Animals of the Sea*. (1910). Oil on canvas, 14 × 9¹/₂″. Collection Mr. and Mrs. Irving W. Schwartz, New York

86

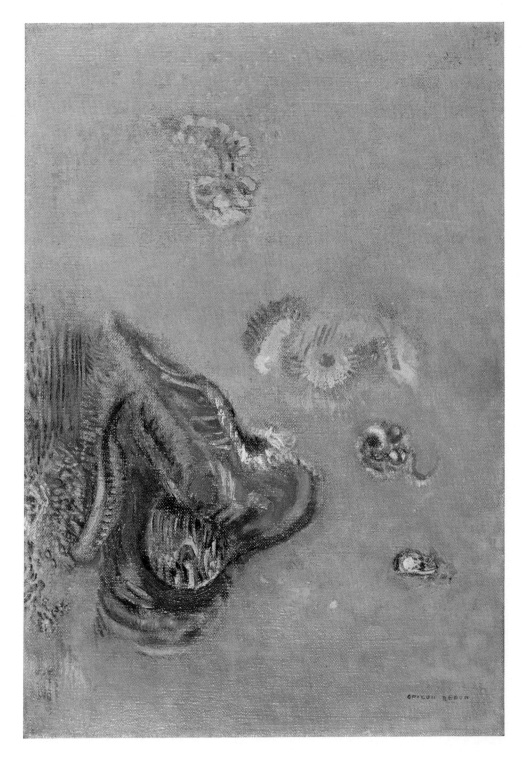

Redon: *Birth of Venus.* (c. 1912). Oil on canvas, 55¹/₂ × 24″. Collection Stephen Higgons, Paris

Redon: *Pandora.* (c. 1910). Oil on canvas, 56¹/₂ × 24¹/₂″. The Metropolitan Museum of Art, New York. Bequest of Alexander Max Bing, 1959

Redon: *Andromeda*. (1912). Oil on canvas, 69×36″. Collection Mr. and Mrs. David Rockefeller, New York

Redon: *Fish*. (1912). Watercolor, 11 × 8⁵/₈″. Collection Mr. and Mrs. Alex M. Lewyt, N. Y.

opposite: Redon: *Sea Anemones*. (c. 1912). Oil on canvas, 20 × 17″. The New Gallery, New York

Redon: *Silence.* (c. 1911). Oil on linen-finish paper, 21¹/₄ × 21¹/₂″. The Museum of Modern Art, New York. The Lillie P. Bliss Collection

opposite: Redon: *Vase of Flowers with Butterflies.* (1912–14). Oil on canvas, 28³/₄ × 21¹/₄″. Private collection, Dallas, Texas, through the courtesy of The Dallas Museum of Fine Arts

Redon: *The Reader*. (1892). Lithograph, $12^{1}/_{4} \times 9^{5}/_{16}''$. The Museum of Modern Art, New York. Gift of Mrs. John D. Rockefeller, Jr.

In 1862, Rodolphe Bresdin had installed himself in the Fosse-aux-lions in Bordeaux (a modern Daniel in the lions' den, he liked to say), and it was there that the young Redon visited him almost daily in the years 1863 to 1865. With Bresdin, Redon felt a bond of sympathy from the very first. He felt at ease as he never had with his teachers, Gorin or Gérôme, who tried to make him do what he knew he could never do well. Redon was particularly captivated by the intimate poetry of Bresdin's etching and under the older master's guidance tried his hand at the copper plate, choosing subjects à la Bresdin, such as knights in desolate mountain landscapes, and working on the same minute scale. Probably his first essay in this medium is *The Ford* of 1865 (Mellerio 2) which he signed in the plate »Odilon Redon, Elève de R. Bresdin," whereas the *Chapel in the Pyrenees*, assigned number 1 and dated 1861 in Mellerio's catalogue, actually bears the date 1866. But even if *The Ford* is close to Bresdin in content and mood, it reveals a different temperament. It is not too happily contained within its small size, and the sharp contrasts of light and shade are conceived in a plastic manner which suggests that the young artist is really thinking in a broader medium. The chiaroscuro effect is even more pronounced in the plate of the *Battling Horsemen* (Mellerio 4), of which we exhibit an undescribed and possibly unique impression, printed before the plate was cut down at the right by about one third. But Redon soon tired of these romantic and heroic subjects, and in one instance, the *Galloping Horseman* (Mellerio 10), he turned the plate right side up, reworked it with the drypoint needle and created the blurred image of a nude woman. This, of course, he may have done many years later, as he

sporadically worked on copper until 1893. *Tobias* (Mellerio 15, c. 1880) is one of those etchings in which Redon is completely himself and no longer the disciple of Bresdin. Gone is the labored tightness of the early plates; it is a delicate and airy vision of great charm, especially in the luminous first state. Redon reworked the plate twice, each time making significant changes. The three impressions exhibited are believed to be unique and came from the artist's own collection of his printed work, which was acquired by The Art Institute of Chicago in 1920.

While Redon practised etching only intermittently (28 etchings are known of which Mellerio described 26), his lithographic work, comprising 197 pieces, leads us directly to the nerve center of his artistic personality. Although Redon has told in *A soi-même* how Bresdin introduced him to lithography at the time of their association in Bordeaux, he did not really begin work in that medium until the late eighteen seventies. His critical attitude to Bresdin's use of lithography is well known: he felt that the minute network of lines created by the pen was not appropriate for the stone. It may well be that he deliberately stayed away from this medium until he had developed a style of drawing grand and bold enough to do justice to it. This he did develop after 1865 and all through the seventies when charcoal became his preferred medium.

In 1898 Redon wrote to Mellerio that it was Fantin-Latour who had introduced him to lithographic crayon and transfer paper and suggested that he reproduce his charcoal drawings by that method. In *A soi-même* (page 121) he wrote: "My first lithographs, published in 1879, were for the most part replicas or variants of drawings which I had made earlier for myself in

Redon: *Tobias* (First state). (c. 1880). 7⁷/₈ × 5³/₄″.
The Art Institute of Chicago. The Stickney Fund

the solitude of the country," thereby referring to *Dans le rêve*, a set of ten lithographs and a frontispiece, published in an edition of only twenty-five copies. Here the language of his symbolism is fully developed, but the handling of the lithographic crayon is still comparatively timid, and the black is only just beginning to assert itself. The same might be said about the portfolios of the early eighties, *À Edgar Poë* (in homage to the American, so revered by the French poets of Redon's generation through the translations of Baudelaire and Mallarmé) which was published in 1882 in fifty copies, and *Les origines,* published in 1883 in twenty-five copies. His style became bolder and at the same time softer and more fluent in the next two portfolios, *Hommage à Goya* (1885) and *La nuit* (1886), both issued in fifty copies. There followed a group of individual lithographs of which the haunting face of Christ and the sarcastically grinning spider are the most remarkable.

In the interpretations—Redon never made "illustrations"—for the monodrama *Le juré* by Picard (1887) and for Flaubert's *Tentation de Saint-Antoine* (1888), as well as for *À Gustave Flaubert* (actually a continuation of the *Tentation*), blacks have become richer and deeper, thereby lending more luminosity to the lighter parts.

In 1889, Redon created *Pegasus Captive,* which has become one of his most celebrated lithographs. It is an especially moving and eloquent version of a subject which played a significant role all through his work, and it is also the ultimate triumph of tonal splendor in mere black and white.

The portfolios of the nineties are *Songes* (1891), the third series of *Tentation de Saint-Antoine* (1896), *La maison hantée* (1896) and *Apocalypse de Saint-Jean* (published by Vollard in 1899). In this last set, Redon employed a wider range of contrasts than ever before: Some plates are conceived in terms of deep, sonorous blacks, others are done in purest outlines and still others in delicate gradations of grey. No less important are the single lithographs of the nineties. *The Reader* (1892) is an affectionate memento of Bresdin. As Mlle Bacou has suggested, Redon portrayed his mentor here in the mood of a philosopher by Rembrandt, the master whom Bresdin had urged him to study above all others. Of the same year is the incredibly delicate and enigmatic mirage of the *Tree* which seems merely breathed upon the paper. Conceived in the same delicate vein is *Brünnehilde* (1894) with her pure and naive Quattrocento profile. (As Sandström pointed out, the Louvre had acquired Pisanello's fa-

Redon: *Fear*. (c. 1865). Etching, $5^{1}/_{2} \times 8^{13}/_{16}$". The Art Institute of Chicago. The Stickney Fund

mous portrait of Ginevra d'Este in 1893.) What a strange interpretation of Wagner's fierce and smoldering heroine!

In the eighteen nineties, color lithography in Paris soared to artistic heights never equalled before or after. Pellet, who published the great color lithographs of Toulouse-Lautrec in 1896–97, and Vollard, who brought out those of Bonnard, Vuillard, Renoir, Roussel and Denis, both applied to Redon, but they got no more from him than one color lithograph each. The frail, elusive charm of *Beatrice*, made for Vollard's *Album des Peintres-Graveurs* of 1897, cannot be denied, but it is in black lithography that Redon speaks most strongly to us. He himself spoke of the sensual distractions of color (though he was a superb colorist), and we know that he respected black as the most essential color and found that especially in lithography it has its "integral and unadulterated force."

As the twentieth century dawned, Redon felt that he had said all he had or cared to say in lithography, and with a series of eight intimate portraits in profile (including Bonnard and Vuillard), he took leave of this medium. If nothing remained of Redon's work except the lithographs, his whole range of thought and emotion, the mysterious and visionary strength and delicacy of his art would still be clearly evident.

HAROLD JOACHIM

Redon: *The Breath that Impels Beings Is also in the Spheres*, Plate V from *À Edgar Poë*. 1882. Lithograph, 10¹¹/₁₆ × 8³/₁₆″. The Art Institute of Chicago. The Stickney Fund

Redon: *The Eye like a Strange Balloon Moves towards Infinity*, Plate I from *À Edgar Poë*. 1882. Lithograph, 10³/₁₆ × 7³/₄″. The Museum of Modern Art, New York. Gift of Peter H. Deitsch.

opposite: Redon: *Eclosion*, Plate I from *Dans le rêve*. 1879. Lithograph, 13¹/₈ × 10¹/₄″. The Art Institute of Chicago. The Stickney Fund

98

99

Redon: *To Old Age*, Plate I from *La nuit*. 1886. Lithograph, 9^1/$_4$ × 7^1/$_4$″.
The Art Institute of Chicago. The Stickney Fund

Redon: *The Swamp Flower, a Sad and Human Face*, Plate II from *Hommage à Goya*. 1885. Lithograph, $10^{13}/_{16} \times 8''$. The Museum of Modern Art, New York. Mrs. John D. Rockefeller, Jr. Purchase Fund

Redon: *Christ*. (1887). Lithograph, $12^7/_8 \times 10^7/_8''$. The Art Institute of Chicago. The Stickney Fund

102

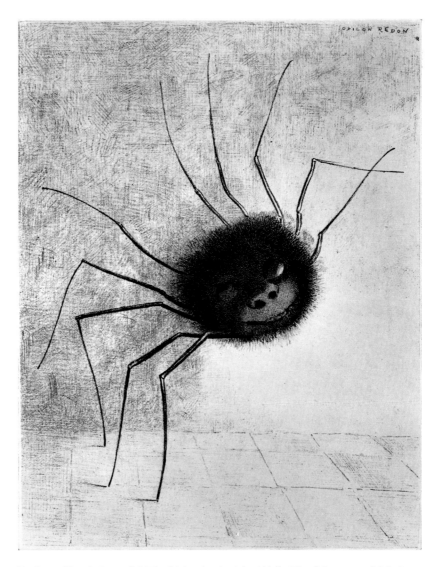

Redon: *The Spider*. (1887). Lithograph, $11 \times 8^{1}/_{2}''$. The Museum of Modern Art, New York. Mrs. Bertram Smith Fund

Redon: *And Below Was the Astral Idol, the Apotheosis*, Plate II from *Songes*. 1891. Lithograph, $10^{7}/_{8} \times 7^{1}/_{2}''$. The Museum of Modern Art, New York. Given anonymously

Redon: *A Skull Was Revealed by the Gap in the Wall*, Plate IV from *Le jurè*. 1887. Lithograph, $9^{3}/_{8} \times 7^{1}/_{4}''$. The Art Institute of Chicago. The Stickney Fund

opposite: Redon: *Pegasus Captive*. (1889). Lithograph, $13^{3}/_{8} \times 11^{5}/_{8}''$. The Museum of Modern Art, New York. The Lillie P. Bliss Collection

104

Redon: *The Light of Day*, Plate VI from *Songes*. 1891. Lithograph, $8^{1}/_{4} \times 6^{1}/_{8}''$. The Museum of Modern Art, New York. The Lillie P. Bliss Collection

Redon: *Anthony: "What Is the Object of all this?"* / *The Devil: "There is no Object."* Plate XVIII from *Tentation de Saint-Antoine*, the third series. 1896. Lithograph, $12^3/_8 \times 9^7/_8''$. The Art Institute of Chicago. The Stickney Fund

108

During his lifetime Gustave Moreau was silent before his critics who condescendingly called him a "literary" painter. Once, however, in a personal letter to a patron, he revealed the chagrin such incomprehension caused him: "I have suffered too much in my life from the unjust and absurd opinion that I am too literary to be a painter."[1]

Long after Moreau's death Georges Rouault wrote an extended essay in which he still felt obliged to defend Moreau from the literary charge.[2] As a student and intimate friend of Moreau, and first curator of the Moreau Museum, Rouault was familiar with the vast secret oeuvre that Moreau had never publicly exhibited. He vehemently insisted that Moreau was too much of a plastic artist, a dreamer, a thinker to stop at the literature of his epoch. "He could talk to me of Baudelaire, of Gerard de Nerval, of Flaubert," he wrote, "he would never think of illustrating works of contemporary literature or of giving in plastic language and color the least equivalence."

Yet in the sum of Moreau's work the literary is undeniably present as are countless other elements, for the mystery of Gustave Moreau is that he pursued not one but many painting ideals, that he followed his imagination determinedly until it brought him to strange junctures that must have startled and baffled even his own lucid intelligence.

If Moreau were seen only in his "literary" works, the Salon pictures with their ambitious allegorical intentions, he would rest in art history as a disconcertingly uneven painter whose dreams were more bizarre than profound. But as Rouault knew so well, Moreau's gifts were dispersed in hidden places. It is in the lesser-known and often unfinished paintings that Moreau the

painterly painter, the uniquely experimental dreamer must be sought and understood.

Far from being the *pompier* the ignorant critics considered him, Moreau was a fervent dissenter from all conventionalized views of painting. He told Rouault that painting could never go back to other centuries, that the "air of the century" necessarily affected the artist.

He knew the limitations of the virtuoso techniques so highly developed in mid-nineteenth-century France. In the precincts of his studio he experimented with radically unorthodox techniques. To his young student Henri Evènepoel he explained that to paint well was not enough. "Even among the masters of virtuosity, the *métier* was not enough to maintain them at the heights equal to the awkward Byzantines who, in a deformed and badly constructed head of a Virgin, elevated themselves to a sentiment of the ideal that has never been surpassed."[3]

Moreau's lifetime was given to the struggle to elevate himself to an almost unapproachable ideal. Born in the Romantic period, his restless mind confronted the problems raised by the new esthetic and, in a sense, carried them to their logical conclusions far in advance of his contemporaries. His inexplicable "abstractions" are as much a reflection of the questions posed by the Romantic generation as are his theatrical presentations of myth and legend. His technical experiments, "discovered" by abstract expressionist artists who find his textures, hectic linear interlaces and strange concordances of color so close to their own, grew as much from Romantic theory milled in his peculiar imagination as did the few large, obsessively detailed "finished" paintings publicly exhibited.

opposite: Moreau: *The Apparition*. Oil on canvas mounted on wood, $12^5/8 \times 9^7/8''$. Musée Gustave Moreau, Paris

A critic of Moreau's own period, Camille Mauclair, recognized the irreconcilable character of the problems Moreau accepted from his cultural heritage. Pointing out that most of the large paintings in the Moreau Museum are unfinished. Mauclair wrote that "in reality, none could have been finished. The means of his painting opposed each other."[4]

Moreau has been seen so variously by critics and connoisseurs that he emerges an invincible figure of paradox. His contemporaries thought of him most often as a "grand malade," though Rouault tells us he was "solid, realistic, without pedantic culture, sometimes lightly sceptical." J.-K. Huysmans, whose *A Rebours* epitomized and caricatured the decadent aspects of estheticism, saw in Moreau's work "the morbid perspicuity of an entirely modern sensibility."[5] He is echoed by André Breton, in the name of Surrealism, who refers admiringly to Moreau's "unhealthy dreams."[6] The American Huneker recognized only Moreau's decorative and theatrical qualities, "he saw ivory, apes and peacocks, purple, gold, and the heavens aflame with a mystic message";[7] Arthur Symons called Moreau "the mathematican of the fantastic, a calculating visionary";[8] Meyer Schapiro considered him a "noble academician";[9] and most recently, Julien Alvard points to the "complex reflections of color and touch" and to "the flights in which matter will be the sole depositary, the sole interpreter."[10]

Which of all these descriptions characterizes Moreau? Clearly he was as Rouault described him, a man interested in everything, of a "curiosity of mind that was never exhausted." He stands in the history of art a symbolic figure, bristling with significant arrows pointing far backward and forward in time, East and West in space.

Moreau's attentiveness to everything, the loyalty he inspired in his students (Matisse and Marquet as well as Rouault), and the loyalty he himself was capable of, according to all his intimate friends, indicates the steadfastness of his character. Through recognizing his moral consistency, his ability to maintain for years ideas and affections formed in his youth, it is possible to enter the climate of his apprentice years despite the paucity of documentation.

He was the son of an architect—a liberal man who, Moreau said, realized the enormous difficulty in judging a work of art, and who never imposed any of his ideas on his son. On the contrary, when Moreau, after two years in the academic studio of François-Edouard Picot (together with Cabanel and Bouguereau) became exasperated and wanted to study with the young Théodore Chasseriau, his father readily consented. Moreau became Chasseriau's student in 1848 when he was twenty-two years old and Chasseriau was only seven years his senior.

Chasseriau not only inspired his pupil through his own exotic quests, but was undoubtedly the medium through which Moreau became aware of the major movements of his time. Chasseriau's importance in Moreau's life, while not explicitly documented, should not be underestimated. He was a precocious, flamboyant personality—born in the Antilles, of striking looks and ardent spirit—whose career began in his early teens. He had been a student of Ingres, became an admirer of Delacroix, and had already won success in the Salon by the time he was twenty.

Chasseriau had entered the art world at the high moment when Romanticism was still vigorously defended by the same band of gifted youths who had fought Victor Hugo's battle of *Hernani*. He was a friend of Théophile Gautier. When Gautier broke away from *Le Petit Cénacle*, the perfervid Romantic group that included Petrus Borel and Gerard de Nerval, to form his own coterie, Chasseriau, then only sixteen, painted two of the murals for Gautier's celebrated 1835 housewarming.[11]

Moreau: *Cavalier*. (c. 1855). Oil on canvas. Musée Gustave Moreau, Paris

Chasseriau, then, experienced the full Romantic sweep and doubtless transmitted its vigor to Moreau. Through Chasseriau Moreau probably met Nerval and some of the outstanding dandys who inspired Baudelaire, encountered the notions of Satanism and Spleen, partook of the spirit of Bohemian revolt, and the art for art's sake devotion that suited his temperament.

Moreau fit easily into the Romantic conception of the artist, for he was above all an "aristocrat" of art, unwilling to make the least concession to bourgeois taste and willing to suffer the consequences. Gautier's 1856 manifesto, summarizing the attitude of his group, may have reflected Moreau's own feelings at the time:

"We believe in the autonomy of art; art for us is not the means but the end; any artist who has in view anything but the beautiful is not an artist in our eyes; we have never been able to understand the separation of idea and form."[12]

Moreau also inherited from the Romantic climate a willingness to endure conflict. Chasseriau's painting conflict—between the untramelled colorism of Delacroix and the pure linearism of Ingres—was passed on to him. Moreau deplored academicism and Salons, but he never wholly abandoned the themes and motifs that were the nineteenth-century painters' stock-in-trade. He was moved by the wildest flights of his poetic and artistic contemporaries, yet himself preferred to stop short before excess. He was drawn to the exoticism represented by the East, studied Persian miniatures and Eastern theologies, but put them in the service of a disciplined, unsentimental conception. The mystic idealism that saturated his period appealed to him. Nevertheless, he scorned theosophical *fin-de-siècle* cults such as the Rosicrucians and remained, as Rouault remarked, something of an eighteenth-century sceptic.

A significant item in Rouault's essay is his allusion to Pascal whom Moreau frequently quoted. The "thought" of Pascal which Moreau copied out for Rouault reflects the sensitive and delicate character of his interest in the mystery of the unknown:

"La connaissance humaine est pareille a une sphère qui grossirait sans cesse a mesure qu'augmente son volume, et grandit le nombre de points de contact avec l'inconnu."[13]

Moreau's religious sentiment was profound but tinged with the wariness of his positivistic century. God, he said, is the immense, and I sense him in me. It was in response to the question: Do you believe in God? that he gave his much-quoted answer:

"I believe only in Him. I don't believe either in that which I touch or that which I see. I believe only in that which I don't see and that which I sense. My brain, my reason seem to me ephemeral and of a doubtful reality. My inner sentiment alone seems to me eternal and incontestably certain."[14]

The complexity and contradictions in Moreau's character, apparent in his work, are indicated by his own statements and those of his most intimate friends whose accounts frequently diverge. Henri Rupp, for one, reported that Moreau always worked in "unquiet haste"[15] while Ary Renan says he "disdained hasty painting."[16] Moreau himself said that his greatest anxiety was to keep a rein on two opposing tendencies in himself: his unbridled imagination and his excessively critical spirit. His sober assessment of old masters had taught him that "the reasonable combination of mind and good sense" must never replace in the artist his "purely plastic imaginative conception."[17]

Despite the evident complexity of Moreau's temperament, critics persist in seeing in him mainly the dark or perverse side. Even in the most recent monograph, Ragnar von Holten sustains his thesis largely with references to Moreau's misogyny, based on his reiterations of themes in which woman—Helen, Salome, Delilah, Circe—appears as the incarnation of evil.[18]

The satanic view of woman, though, can be seen more properly as a conventional view of the Romantic movement. The symbolic idea of woman as bewitcher

Moreau: *Oedipus and the Sphinx*. 1864. Oil on canvas, 81¹/₈ × 41¹/₄″. The Metropolitan Museum of Art, New York. Bequest of William H. Herriman, 1921

113

haunted Baudelaire, Alfred de Vigny, Barbey d'Aure-villy, Leconte de Lisle, Flaubert, Schopenhauer, Mallarmé and scores of other major nineteenth-century figures. As a theme the wily temptress was rich and inexhaustible. Artists of the period found her too tempting artistically to resist.

Moreau encountered her again and again from his early youth. Gérard de Nerval published *Les Chimères* in 1854. Chasseriau was still alive and chances are that Moreau knew it through Chasseriau's enthusiasm. Woman, said Nerval, is the Chimera of man, or, if you like, his demon. We know that Moreau read Alfred de Vigny assiduously. De Vigny's *La Colère de Samson* is close indeed to Moreau's thought:[19]

"An eternal struggle in all times, all places
takes place on earth in the presence of God
between the goodness of Man and the wiles of Woman
for woman is an impure being in body and soul"

It is in this poem that the famous line "And, more or less, Woman is always DELILAH" occurs. (While Schopenhauer wrote that "every hero is a Samson.")

Fear of the degrading and sapping influences of sensuousness, of *volupté*, runs consistently through nineteenth-century literature and philosophy. Bourgeois morality encouraged the split between "love" and "sensuality," and many young spirits were shaped by it. Without going into psychological excavation, it is possible to see how in the cases of de Vigny, Flaubert, and Moreau—all exceptionally devoted to their mothers—the ideal of purity was inevitably opposed to sex and sensuousness. Raised to a principle, Woman became for Moreau and certain of his contemporaries, Nature—the inscrutable, mindless force with which Man must do battle in order to realize his superiority.

Man for Moreau and his romantic colleagues was epitomized by the Artist. Art was an exalted ideal to which the artist sacrificed everything. It was a sustained dream, a struggle to envision some transcending synthesis of all human emotion and thought. The correspondences of sight, smell, sound suggested by Baudelaire ultimately led to correspondences of intangibilia throughout the universe.

Marcel Proust understood Moreau's artistic hegira, the full meaning of his sustained dream. He thought that Moreau tried to break down the barrier of the individual "I." Moreau was, Proust wrote, "one of those who have an inner soul into which they can sometimes penetrate. The rest of their life is a kind of exile, often voluntary, not sad but tedious."[20]

Moreau's own observations, written in his notebooks, frequently in order to share his thoughts with his mother who had become deaf, bear Proust out. Above all, his attitude is reflected in his will, an important document in the mystery of Moreau.

In the will Moreau requested that the state "keep as long as possible this collection, conserving its character as an ensemble which shows the sum of work and the effort of the artist during his life."

The idea of making an ensemble of the emblems of his working imagination occurred to Moreau early in his career. It appears that he personally installed the hundreds of oil paintings and thousands of watercolors and drawings in elaborate cabinets opening out like Chinese puzzles; in the walls throughout his house which fold upon themselves like accordions; in the revolving *meuble* occupying the largest of his two studios on the top floor.

On the eve of his death he is said to have gone over hundreds of his drawings signing and lightly correcting them. He saw his life as the works it engendered—the "machine" paintings as well as the enigmatic abstractions.

Among the works carefully mounted by Moreau and honored in the vast repository of his imagination were drawings made on his extended trip to Italy in 1857—landscapes of the Roman campagna, views of Florence and environs similar in style to Corot, copies of frescoes and murals, and studies of decorative details. His admiration for the Venetians—not just Carpaccio whom he copied faithfully, but Veronese and Titian as well— was matched by his enthusiasm for Michelangelo, Mantegna, Leonardo da Vinci and Luini. During this voyage, on which he encountered Degas and Puvis de Chavannes, Moreau stored volumes of imagery in his notebooks. He used them repeatedly later.

Italy's immediate impact appeared in his first works to be widely discussed—works shown at the Salons of 1864 and 1865, in both of which he won medals. Hostile critics accurately noted his eclectic tendency, remarking on his naive pedantry of Renaissance lore, his attempt to translate Greece in fourteenth-century Tuscan dialect, his retrograde instincts. One jeered at *Young Man and Death*, dedicated to Chasseriau, as "a pastiche of Mantegna made by a German student who is resting from painting by reading Schopenhauer."[21]

If we look at *Oedipus and the Sphinx*, exhibited in 1864, from the distance of a century, Moreau's antagonists seem justified. The painting is dull in color— the grays and tans under glaze so typical of academicians. It is filled with annoying accumulations of naturalistic detail not very far from the vulgar naturalism of M. Picot himself.

The theme obviously springs from the literature of the period, summarized by Edouard Schuré: "Since time immemorial, Nature, seductive, inscrutable, is the queen of man. Nature, symbolized by the Sphinx, eventually is outwitted by man and plunges into the abyss. Thus, nature penetrated in the hierarchy of her forces is defeated by man who incorporates and surpasses her in thinking."[22]

Moreau's handling of the theme impressed many of his viewers. In revolt against the anecdotal acting-out of the drama (and didn't Moreau scorn David's gesturing personages, calling his paintings "tableaux vivants"?) he was already in search of a way to suggest rather than describe.

Moreau: *Sketch B*. Oil on cardboard, 15³/₄ × 12¹/₂″. Musée Gustave Moreau, Paris

The two mythical figures gaze at each other transfixed. This is characteristic of Moreau who again and again suggests an ambiguous mirror-image, two aspects, two abstract entities that confront each other and recognize each other all too well.

Another typical vision is the fantasy of mountains, great rocky eminences that close in the action and describe the abyss always threatening the characters in Moreau's mythology. Mountains are often transformed into towers or thrones in his paintings, and seem to symbolize an ideal of ascension for Moreau.

Moreau: *Salome Dancing before Herod.* (c. 1870). Oil on canvas, 55¹/₂ × 41″. Collection Huntington Hartford, New York

opposite: Moreau: *Hercules and the Hydra of Lerne.* (c. 1876). Oil on canvas, 70³/₄ × 60³/₄″. Collection Richard L. Feigen, Chicago

117

The static drama of confrontation recurs in *Hercules and the Hydra of Lerne* that together with the most famous of Moreau's many versions of *Salome* electrified the Salon of 1876. Moreau was then fifty years old, and the principles of his art were well established. Hercules, the "destroyer of monsters," symbolic combatant against death, is seen calm and meditative in a crepuscular landscape. His androgynous body suggests not the burly adventurer of late antiquity but the sensitive artist-poet. (Of another painting Moreau wrote that "the destroyer of monsters waits, meditates this great act of generation; he feels the immense sadness of him who is going to create, to give Life, at the same time as the great exaltation of soul which strikes him, the devotée of sacrifices, in each act of his fatal destiny.")[23]

The strange combination of fantasy, particularly in the landscape, and pedantic naturalism—the hydra is compiled from meticulous snake studies Moreau made in the Jardin des Plantes—drew the admiring attention of several critics. With *Salome* it established Moreau's style as it was to be known to the public of his time.

This public image of Moreau's style was intelligently reflected in the monograph written by Ary Renan and published, in 1900, only a year after Moreau's death.[24] Renan makes several significant points in his commentary. He warns of the futility of trying to establish a chronology. Moreau carried his obsessions along for years, reworked canvases constantly, and sometimes revised paintings more than thirty years after they were begun.

Moreau's two guiding principles, according to Renan, who claimed he heard Moreau discourse on them frequently, were the principles of *la belle inertie* and *la richesse nécessaire*. The idea of beautiful inertia, the psychological suspension found in Moreau's Salon paintings, must have occured to him rather early. Renan

quotes him as admiring Michelangelo's "ideal somnambulism" in the Sistine Chapel. Necessary richness on a simple level refers to Moreau's almost manic need to accumulate lapidary detail. But other remarks of Moreau, particularly those directed against painting as decoration, indicate that Renan took these principles too literally and overemphasized them. It is possible, too, that they represented Moreau's thoughts at one period in his life and were subsequently modified. Moreau's unfinished late works contradict these two much-quoted principles which seem to apply only to the "finished" work Moreau exhibited and sold to his small group of faithful patrons.

In another passage Renan points to a more inclusive principle that fits more readily Moreau's ideal of a synthesis of all sensation and thought:

"His idea was to equal, without deranging the harmony of line, and by the prestige alone of environing decoration, all the suggestions provoked in literature, music, and the theatre."

This comes very close to the Wagnerian ideal hovering over French arts since first Gérard de Nerval and later Baudelaire discovered Wagner. (Moreau was a music lover himself and boasted to his students that in his youth he could sing all the Wagner operas.) In his later work, interest in abstract or "musical" aspects of composition becomes dominant. But in *Hercules* and *Salome*, Renan's two principles still apply.

Moreau's elaboration of the principle of *richesse nécessaire* as quoted by Renan is open both to literal and figurative interpretation:

"Whether they were from Flanders, Hungary, Venice or Cologne, the masters strove to create a universe transcending the real ... What cities Carpaccio or Memling built for St. Ursula! ... What valleys hollowed out of sapphire are opened by the Lombard painters! ... On the walls of museums, how many windows are opened on artificial worlds which seem carved from marble and gold, and from spaces *necessarily* chimerical!"

Moreau's *Salome* and its numerous variants embodies these ideas. Using realistic detail—as did Flaubert when he built his word-poem Salammbô which corresponds so closely to Moreau's image—and with fanciful arabesques and arcane symbols, Moreau carved his artificial world from chimerical spaces.

According to von Holten, Moreau filled his composition with signs of sensuality and perversity. "Salome has in her hand the lotus, symbol of voluptuousness.

Moreau: *St. Cecilia.* Oil on canvas, 33⁷/₈ × 26³/₄". Musée Gustave Moreau, Paris

Herodiade, her mother, incarnate Vice, is holding a fan of peacock feathers. Finally, the background is dominated by an imposing Diane of Ephesus, goddess of Fecundity."

The Salome, then, does not depart from the traditional Romantic image of woman as the principle of evil. The painting, however, is a distinct and original departure from Moreau's early style. His taste for elaborate architectural detail is indulged to the full, yet always within a grandiose tectonic scheme carefully balanced. The great pillars of light that so moved Moreau, and are seen in many of the smaller sketches, come from the golden depths of the picture. Chiaroscuro effects, possibly studied in Rembrandt, are stressed. (Moreau's interest in Rembrandt may have been stimulated by his great friend, the critic, novelist, and painter, Eugène Fromentin, who visited him frequently.)

Delilah, Helen, Europa, Leda, Pasiphaë—these legendary women appear in Moreau's paintings again and again, treated in radically different manners. He even painted Salome in modern dress, a watercolor of extraordinary freshness. Delilah was depicted as a sultry cousin to Moreau's own Salomé, or as a reflection of one of Rembrandt's bathing women, or as a sympathetic Oriental seductress. The small oil sketch of Delilah in repose is a delicate and original vision, closer to a Whistler "arrangement" than a decadent illustration. Light from behind, always fascinating to Moreau, is divided off into screenlike planes that recur in numerous oil sketches. In this instance, he is not painting with the misogynist's spite, but rather with tenderness.

There is at least one quotation, resembling a statement of de Vigny, in which Moreau's detachment and potential sympathy are voiced. "Fatal lovers," he says of his cast of treacherous women, "condemned ones of titanic shames, what will become of you, what terrors, what pities you inspire!"[25]

Moreau: *Salome*. Watercolor, 15 × 9³/4″. Musée Gustave Moreau, Paris

Moreau: *Delilah*. Oil on canvas, 12^{1}/$_{8}$ × 15^{3}/$_{4}$″. Musée Gustave Moreau, Paris

His own special note of redemption for his feminine sinners is struck again in one of the strangest of his teeming allegorical paintings, *The Chimeras* with the sub-title, *Satanic Decameron*.

The picture is signed and dated 1884 though it is "unfinished." Here, Moreau threw in his entire cast of ill-starred women. Leaning more toward symbolism than classical allegory (in the sense that the characters do not make a charade of their histories, but are there to suggest broader underlying motifs) Moreau builds them into a complicated human architecture that ascends toward apotheosis. To understand this facet of Moreau's revery, it is worth reading his own description to the full:

"This island of fantastic dreams encloses all forms of passion, fantasy and caprice in the woman, woman in her primary essence, the unconscious being fond of the unknown, the mysterious, in love with evil in the form of a perverse and diabolic seduction. The dreams of children, of the senses, monstrous dreams, melancholy dreams, dreams that carry the spirit and the soul into the unknown spaces, into the mystery of gloom, everything must experience the influence of the seven deadly sins, everything is found in these satanic precincts in this circle of the vices and the guilty ardors, from the as yet innocent germ to the monstrous and fatal flowers of the abyss. . . . These are the theories of damned queens who have just left the serpent; these are beings in which the soul is abolished, waiting at the side of the road for the lewd goat mounted by Luxury to adore his passage: isolated beings, somber in their dreams of desire, of unsatiated pride, in their bestial isolation. Women astride Chimeras who carry them into space where they fall again, lost in horror and vertigo.

"The dark, terrible, mortal Chimeras, Chimeras of Space, of Water, of Mystery, of the Shadow and of the Dream.

Moreau: Study (probably for *The Chimeras*). (Begun in 1884). Watercolor, 12¹/₂ × 9″. Musée Gustave Moreau, Paris

Moreau: *The Chimeras (Satanic Decameron)*. Detail

Moreau: *The Chimeras (Satanic Decameron)*. 1884. Oil on canvas, 92⁷/₈ × 80¹/₄″. Musée Gustave Moreau, Paris

"In the distance, the dead town with dormant passions.

"And this town, which is real life, true life, that which is hidden enclosed within somber walls under low roofs.

"But the mountainous roads, the narrow roads rise, and figures spaced out, climb with difficulty toward the summits, tired, panting, bleeding figures, they mount always clinging to the sharp points of this arid and barren rock. And perhaps in this ardent effort, in despair, perhaps they will succeed in elevating themselves enough so that they will only see the sky in its limpid and pure zenith—Perhaps they will arrive at the redemptory cross that rises humbly in the Ether, last stop of Life, last evidence of what is creative and beneficent, last refuge of the Being who has been able to avoid or vanquish the visionary dream after cruel afflications, the terrible dream of ruin, sorrow, and death."[26]

If the pejorative meaning of the term "literary painter" holds at all, it applies to this bizarre picture. The idea was present before Moreau began his painting. The documentation included not only a replica of a Northern Gothic city, undoubtedly taken from an old engraving, but all manner of eclectic detail. Rembrandt, Giorgione, Gozzoli, millefleurs tapestries, Greek vases—there was no end to Moreau's sources.

This visual lexicon, section by section, synopsizes Moreau's obsessions.

In general he was not greatly moved by the female nude. His numerous studies from the model, sometimes accompanied with pencil notations of her traits and her address, were stiff, often poor in observation. But when he let his fantasy move away from the perceived figure, Moreau could trace the firm outlines of general femininity with considerable style. In several of the figures in *The Chimeras*, drawn in ink on the canvas, his bold contour line suggests not only Matisse, but Picasso in his classic period figures.

When Moreau takes up his other favorite theme—the tragic poet—he invariably simplifies his means. The poet-painter in himself, chary of "logic and good sense" assumes the dominant voice. The creator-hero is almost always seen in a melancholy landscape with a heavy orange or white sun sinking rapidly behind him, the sun being, in Moreau's words, the emblem of virile force.

Hesiod, Oedipus, Theseus, Hercules, David, and Prometheus appear as the poet, the Being charged with a tragically unequal combat with Nature. It was Orpheus, however, who most stirred Moreau's imagination.

Orpheus released in him a sentiment that went well beyond the mere representation of an idea. His *Orpheus at the Tomb of Eurydice* never publicly exhibited and undated, though probably belonging to his last years, is wholly different from the learned allegories.

Here Orpheus is placed in a somber landscape, his lyre hung on a tree stump, his head lowered in contemplation. Imprisoned in this mournful locale by a dark green lake, the shadowed and lightly sketched Greek temple, and the fringe of trees, he symbolizes the solitary and agonizing role of the artist, one Moreau felt to be his own.

It is largely through the paint itself that Moreau conjures the pervasive atmosphere of sadness. Moreau's contemporaries would have recoiled before the red-madder trees hemming in the foreground. Not until the Fauves were non-naturalistic colors used so daringly. These trees Moreau laid on with a hasty palette knife, turning and twisting his strokes to suggest the density of leafage, and painting the fringes in a lighter red to trap the last light of the sinking white sun. Above the trees, a turbid white-to-deep-blue sky suggests the coldness of dying day.

Coldness, light that has no warmth and serves to isolate the human being was a specialty of Moreau's. We

Moreau: *Orpheus at the Tomb of Eurydice*. Oil on canvas, 68¹/₂ × 50³/₈", Musée Gustave Moreau, Paris find opaque cascades of unreal light in a number of his paintings (among them *The Good Samaritan* and *Ganymede)*. Sometimes the light is painted with the full side of the palette knife in planes that resemble the planes of Courbet. It is as if Moreau wanted to suggest that even light can be impenetrable. It becomes yet another element against which man must struggle.

In *Orpheus* the importance of the light is emphasized by the lake below handled with a rapid brush. The

Moreau: *The Rat from the City and the Rat from the Country*. Sketch for "The Fables of La Fontaine." (c. 1881). Watercolor, 11³/₈ × 8¹/₄″. Musée Gustave Moreau, Paris

freedom of dense cross-strokes, so notable in the last years, can only have come from an emotional release, an inspired realization of the "dreamed" color, the "pure plastic means" which stood on the one side of Moreau's esthetic.

The incipient expressionism in this painting, even more apparent in the wild Euripidean fantasies such as the *Circe* was possibly nurtured by Moreau's watercolor experiments. Watercolor was the realm in which he allowed himself the most license.

The problem of dating is simplified in the case of Moreau's watercolors by the fact the Anthony Roux commissioned him to do illustrations for "The Fables of La Fontaine" in 1881. Rouault considered the suite of sixty-five watercolors Moreau's best works, and used them to support his argument that Moreau was not a literary painter. There is scarcely a direct illustration. The ensemble includes meticulously rendered decorative fantasies, rough expressionist studies, chiaroscuro images, and delicate compositions influenced by Persian miniatures.

Moreau labored for almost five years on these watercolors. In the course of his concentrated work the mature painter—he was now nearing sixty—came closer to his brush and painted more directly. Probably this cycle led him into the extraordinary experiences represented by such watercolors as *Narcissus, Les lyres mortes, The Temptation of St. Anthony* and *The Combat of the Centaurs.*

It is in the watercolors, and a few of the oil sketches, that Moreau's intuition of the plastic use of abstraction is best revealed. In them he could dream the large diffuse dreams, dreams of the Chimeras of Space, of Water, of Shadow, of Dream. In them he could relinquish his lexicon of assigned symbols in favor of floating cosmic visions so nearly like the visions of today's abstract painters. Detail surrenders to the generality; allegory to mystery; representation to suggestion. The very characteristics that Manet reproach-

Moreau: *Ganymede*. Watercolor, 9³/₄ × 13³/₄″. Musée Gustave Moreau, Paris

128

Moreau: *Circe*. Oil on canvas, 18¹/₈ × 15¹/₄″. Musée Gustave Moreau, Paris

opposite: Moreau: *Thomyris and Cyrus*. Oil on canvas, 23⁵/₈ × 35³/₈″. Musée Gustave Moreau, Paris.

130

Moreau: *Phaeton*. (Before 1878). Watercolor, 13¹/₂ × 10″.
Musée Gustave Moreau, Paris

Moreau: *Polyphemus*. Oil on canvas, 18¹/₈ × 10″. Musée Gustave
Moreau, Paris

opposite: Moreau: *The Death of Inspiration (Les lyres
mortes)*. (c. 1895–97). Watercolor, 15 × 9³/₄″. Musée Gustave
Moreau, Paris

131

ed Moreau for ("I have a lively sympathy for him, but he is taking a bad road ... He takes us back to the incomprehensible, while we wish that everything be understood")[27] are the elements which bring Moreau so close to the contemporary sensibility.

Théophile Gautier linked Moreau with Edgar Allan Poe, and though Moreau seemed to consider Poe excessively morbid, he shared with the American poet a deep need to pass beyond petty mortal details of human existence into a dreamed Paradise which represented cosmic unity. Throughout Poe's tales and poems, the protagonists strain toward an abstract realm midway between dream and revery. His imagery, much like Moreau's, is keyed to closure. The landscape of *The Domain of Arnheim* with its "funeral gloom," its gorges and abysses, its impenetrable walls of foliage, is the landscape that encloses Moreau's tragic poets.

In his notebooks Moreau made several references to an *au delà abstrait* which stood for him as an ideal that he hardly hoped to approach. Since this abstract realm divests itself of the specific flora, fauna, objects and personages existing in the concrete or known world, only a general image could suggests its transcendence. The "subjects," so remote from language that mid-twentieth-century painters tried to paint in visual form, are not distant from the "subjects" that Moreau evoked either consciously or inadvertently in his freest sketches.

Among the watercolors, *Narcissus*, which von Holten dates toward 1895, is a prodigy of unorthodox technique. Who before Moreau had thought of squeezing impasto threads of color directly from the tube? Who had applied the whiplashes of greens, blues and scarlets in such intricate mazes? And who had used the rough tooth of the paper to break the flow of watercolor movement, to make the forms recede and charge forward beneath the dry-brush touches spread rhythmically throughout the painting?

The figure of Narcissus is deliberately vague, a body transparent like a lake or mirror. Trails of red traverse his body. He lives in the swampy grotto of consuming Nature, the aqueous suspension that so appealed to Moreau that Galatea became one of his most frequent themes.

Scraping, impasto, clotting, threading, dragged brush and linear fury: audacious and unprecedented means toward an increasingly abstract end. Even more in the *Temptation of St. Anthony* and the *Combat of the Centaurs*, Moreau's need to express the themes in terms of matter itself predominates. Horizons, perspective recessions vanish. Color—Moreau's favorite reds, deep blues and greens—is set free and used to express sentiments inspired indirectly by the motif.

Even when at the end of his life Moreau resumed his ambitious themes, as in *Les lyres mortes (The Death of Inspiration)*, the "idea" receded, the impulse of his hand and the poetry of line and color took over. At such times he may have appeared to himself as his own image of Phaeton, rushing through unknown skies toward his tragic end, experiencing for a few moments the exhilaration of the spheres, hurtling among reeling orbs and knowing the Chaos Redon thought Moreau so perfectly described in his famous watercolor *Phaeton*.[28] (Redon wrote, "This Phaeton is a conception full of daring that has for its object the representation of Chaos ... There is in the magnificence of these nuances, in the audacious divergence of lines, in the harshness and caustic quality of these vivid colors, a grandeur, an emotion and somehow, a new wonder.")

The preliminary watercolor study for *Les lyres mortes* is signed and titled by Moreau. According to von Holten it was painted between 1895 and 1897. The theme is a synopsis of many earlier paintings. As in the previous works, Moreau had a specific verbal analogue for his conception:

"The poets, pagan chanters, die of this embrace, of this ardent communion with matter under the forms

Moreau: *Narcissus*. Watercolor, $20^7/8 \times 24''$. Musée Gustave Moreau, Paris

Moreau: *The Temptation of St. Anthony*. (c. 1890). Watercolor, 5¹/₈×9³/₈″. Musée Gustave Moreau, Paris

opposite: Moreau: *Combat of the Centaurs*. Watercolor.
5⁷/₈×11″. Musée Gustave Moreau, Paris

Moreau: *Galatea*. Oil and gouache on canvas, 14⁵/₈ × 10³/₈″.
Collection Mr. and Mrs. Harold X. Weinstein, Chicago

Moreau: *Galatea*. (c. 1880). Oil on wood, 33³/₈ × 26³/₈″. Collection Robert Lebel, Paris

136

Moreau: *Galatea*. (c. 1895). Oil on canvas,
90¹/₄ × 47¹/₄″. Musée Gustave Moreau, Paris

created by them: Hamadryads, Naiads, Sources, Wood Nymphs; of this immersion in vegetative nature, of this maddening, delirious union of hopeless hyper-sensitivity, with this mute, insensible nature, taking, dying without cease to be reborn more vital, absorbing everything around it, serene, silent, full of mystery, animated, penetrated, created living by the imagination, the adoration, the lyre of the pagan poet. But the great lyre of the soul, the great voice with vibrating chords of an ideal truly divine comes to stifle, to abolish all these voices of the senses, these voices of glorified nature; it rises, this superb lyre, held by a somber and terrible archangel, armed with a cross of blood that will regenerate the world, this sublime cross, symbol of sacrifice, of distrust of ephemeral things and witness supreme of adoration of the Eternal divine.

"The great Ocean of the antique centuries draws in a powerful reflux these stars once brilliant which die in somber waters, and all these worlds of thought, of earthly poetry disappear, submerged by the punishing flood, avenger and redemptor of the divine Ideal."[29]

A resounding edifice of words that resembles Moreau's earlier word pictures. But the paintings, both watercolor and oil, are leagues away. There are only the barest traces of poet, cross, lyre and deity in the watercolor. Instead, floats of blue, green, orange move in criss-cross patterns: the elements rather than their mythological symbols. Three suns and their reflections sink into the waters. Brackish horizontals cover them. Spots of scarlet and green, unrelated except in a "musical" way, draw the touches and strokes together in an abstract surface pattern.

When he came to paint the oil, which though it appears unfinished may have satisfied the artist, Moreau carried over the staccato technique. A dim orange sky is crossed with scrubby white and black horizontals. Sun shapes and halo shapes are reiterated throughout. Detached red spots, like blots, occur in regular inter-vals all over the surface. Blackish-purple lines in complex calligraphic tracery move beneath the surface.

The same technical peculiarities occur in *Galatea*, possibly painted around the same time. Her white body is set in a welter of little touches of color. Thick blobs, scrapings from the paletteknife, alternate with very thin, almost running passages. Reds and blues are played down in somber contrasts, and the white of the canvas seems deliberately exposed.

Possibly Moreau intended to overpaint and "finish" this canvas. But it is conceivable too, that it struck him as a just expression of an aspect of Galatea's myth that most interested him at the time. In other, earlier versions, the specific details of her story are carefully rendered. Here, Moreau is concerned with the general atmosphere, the sad circumstance and mood of her being, and the meditative posture of Polyphemus.

It is not difficult to make a transition from the late thematic paintings to the smaller watercolors and oils in which either no identifiable subject exists, or, exists so ambiguously that it verges on abstraction. There are some two hundred of them preserved, and their meaning has been vigorously disputed. Some critics maintain that they were merely trial sketches for "passages" in the larger paintings. Others think they are "unfinished" ideas that Moreau himself would not have considered seriously.

The fact remains that Moreau regarded them seriously enough to frame and mount. Although they are not dated, the freedom of technique relates them to his last works. It is certainly possible that in his last years, Moreau, a secretive man whose intense inner life was carefully guarded, embarked on a compelling adventure in which even he, with all his "excessive critical power" could not immediately find the meaning. When people spoke to him of the decadence of painting, Rupp reports that Moreau answered, "They say it is finished. It is just beginning!"[30]

Moreau: *Sketch D.* Oil on cardboard, 18¹/₂ × 12¹/₂″. Musée Gustave Moreau, Paris

Moreau: *Sketch E*. Oil on wood, $12^5/8 \times 9^7/8''$. Musée Gustave Moreau, Paris

Moreau: *Sketch A*. Oil on wood, $8^5/_8 \times 10^5/_8''$. Musée Gustave Moreau, Paris

In a sense these renditions of the elements, of pure light effects, clouds, rushes of water, are reflections not only of Moreau's own speculations, but of the thoughts that sporadically break through in nineteenth-century notations by painters and poets.

Delacroix spoke in his journal of a "kind of emotion particularly proper to painting" which results from arrangements of colors, lights and shadows. "This is called the music of the picture." Probably prompted by Delacroix, Baudelaire developed his own theory of musicality in painting. Beyond "correspondences" of colors, sounds and sights, aptly exaggerated in Huysmans' portrait of des Esseintes, Baudelaire understood that there was a unity peculiar to the plastic arts that had nothing to do with the subject the painter depicted. "A well-drawn figure penetrates you with a joy that is entirely alien to the subject. Voluptuous or terrible, this figure owes its charm to the arabesque it cuts out in space."[31] Recurrent reflection on the "musicality" in painting and the "arabesque" undoubtedly impressed Moreau who was susceptible to all imaginative speculation. After Delacroix, many had toyed with the idea of detaching the emotional values of color and line from specific objects, and although it remained for Kandinsky to put these speculations to the visual test, the pre-existence of the theories must be acknowledged.

These scattered symbolist intuitions received fuller expression only in the 1880s when, in the newly-founded *Revue Wagnérienne*, many essayists attempted to sort out the relationships of music and poetry and painting.

In 1886, Teodor de Wyzewa, editor of the review, wrote of an "emotional art, a musical art, overlooking the objects that colors and lines represent, taking them solely as signs of emotions." He praised the *peintres symphonistes* and asserted that "art must recreate ... by means of signs, the total life of the universe, that is to say, of the soul where the variegated drama we call the universe is played."[32]

Wyzewa's synthesizing idealism corresponds to Moreau's—Moreau who referred so often to the "arabesque" in its ideal, universalizing connotation, opposing it to mind and good sense.

The arabesque as plastic equivalent to the soul in all its mystery was discussed by many artists and poets. Mallarmé, to whom Moreau has been compared by more than one critic, posited the arabesque with particularly arcane implications. Like Moreau he alluded constantly to Chimeras, and, like Moreau, his passion as an artist was to penetrate the depths of his own soul. He scorned naturalism and spoke again and again of an abstract arabesque:

"We conjure up a scene of lovely, evanescent, intersecting forms. We recognize the entire binding arabesque thus formed as it leaps dizzily in terror or plays disquieting chords, or through a sudden digression (by no means disconcerting) we are warned of its likeness unto itself even as it hides."[33]

In a letter to Gustave Kahn he wrote that "anyone who has a sense of musical structure can listen to his own particular and inward arabesques of sound."[34]

Not arabesques of sound but arabesques of line and color preoccupied Moreau. In the early work, the "arabesque" was literally that of line which he had studied in Greek and Oriental art. But later, the arabesque becomes the abstraction Mallarmé described. Even in Moreau's epic theogonies, his attempts to bring together all human experience—the myths of the East and of the Bible and of antiquity—so that they became a single cosmic unity, the idea of this abstract arabesque is implicit.

Who, looking at the small oils, could deny that the experience of "abstract" color and movement absorbed Moreau completely? In one (*Sketch A*) a flaming red shape—rose or figure?—is pulled out from the material by the artist's fingers. His thumb prints are clear. In another (*Sketch C*) clouds of green and blue, flecks of dispersed color are there because Moreau

Moreau: *Sketch C*. Oil on canvas, $10^5/_8 \times 8''$. Musée Gustave Moreau, Paris "felt" them in purely plastic terms. Color in all the enigmatic oil sketches, and in several of the abstract watercolors, is applied with evident passion, completely released from its signifying connotations. Whether or not Moreau thought of himself as painting the *au delà abstrait*, the fact remains that he instinctively used abstract means adumbrated in the nineteenth century and realized in the twentieth.

Baudelaire said that the artist stems only from himself and dies childless.[35] Huysmans, speaking of Moreau, said he was nobody's pupil with no real ancestors and no possible descendants.[36] Alvard says flatly that Moreau was no precursor, if he made abstract paintings it was inadvertently.[37]

But if Moreau died childless, he left behind him an enigma so tantalizing, so full of significant clues that countless artists and writers have been tempted to try to find entry to his hermetic art.

His students praised his broad spirit. Matisse credited his prophetic abilities when he repeated that Moreau had told him that he, Matisse, was destined to simplify painting.[38] Rouault never tired of rendering homage to Moreau's unlimited culture and his profound understanding of painting, *all* painting. Both knew Moreau at the end of his life when, in 1892, he became professor at the Ecole des Beaux-Arts. The young artists were exposed to Moreau's mature reflections rather than the traditional views of his romantic youth.

Rouault pointed out that Moreau had at least an intuition of the advanced aspects of his own work. "I am the bridge over which certain of you will pass" he told Rouault. He knew that he could not look to his own epoch for complete understanding and mentioned several times that he hoped to find understanding with posterity. To console Rouault, he told him: "Solitude, happy obscurity in the face of the incomprehension of people who defend the formulas of success, all that has its good side." And he added, half laughing, half serious, "When they don't like what you do, you have the advantage of being able to expand and develop yourself freely; I wish you late success; you won't then undergo any depressing influence. ..."[39]

The Moreau Museum, hermetic as the personality of Moreau himself, has been "discovered" at regular intervals since his death. Kandinsky is reported to have visited it as early as 1906.[40] André Breton writes that he "discovered" the museum when he was sixteen years old (and has claimed Moreau for the Surrealist pantheon ever since). Countless artists and writers during the past ten years have entered its musty chambers in search of the Moreau who was said to have painted so nearly like the *tachistes* or abstract expressionists.

Bridge, unique visionary, precursor? There is no answer. Moreau's mysteries assure him a unique position in the history of modern art.

DORE ASHTON

1 Catalogue of the Musée Gustave Moreau, 1926. The passage continues: "Whatever I write to you about my picture, in order to please you, need not be explained in words; the sense of this painting for those who know a little how to read a plastic creation is extremely clear and limpid. ..."

2 Georges Rouault, "Gustave Moreau," *L'Art et les Artistes*, vol. XII, 1926, p. 220.

3 Henri Evènepoel, *Gustave Moreau et ses Elévès*, Lettres d'Henri Evènepoel à son père, Paris, Ed. Michel, 1923.

4 Camille Mauclair, *De Watteau à Whistler*, Paris, 1905.

5 Joris-Karl Huysmans, *A Rebours* translated by Robert Baldick as *Against Nature*, London, Penguin Books, 1959, p. 69.

6 André Breton, *L'Art Magique*, Paris, 1957.

7 James Gibbons Huneker, *Promenades of An Impressionist*, New York, 1910, p. 348–356.

8 Arthur Symons, *Studies in Seven Arts*, London, 1910.

9 Meyer Schapiro, "Fromentin As A Critic," *Partisan Review*, vol: 16, January, 1949, pp. 25–51.

10 Julien Alvard, Catalogue for the exhibition "Antagonismes" at the Musée des Arts Decoratifs, February, 1960, p. 43.

11 Enid Starkie, *Petrus Borel, The Lycanthrope*, Norfolk, Conn., New Directions, 1954, p. 124. Appropriately enough, Chasseriau painted a group of Bacchantes. Miss Starkie notes that when Gautier's house was being torn down, Gerard de Nerval rescued some of the paintings, among them Chasseriau's Bacchantes.

12 Théophile Gautier, "Introduction," *L'Artiste*, Paris, Dec. 14, 1856.

13 Rouault, *op. cit.*, p. 231.

14 *ibid.*, p. 240.

15 Cited by Léon Deshairs and Jean Laran, *Gustave Moreau*, Paris, 1913.

16 Ary Renan, "Gustave Moreau," Paris, *Gazette des Beaux-Arts*, 1899.

17 Cited by Ragnar von Holten, *Gustave Moreau*, Paris, Pau-

vert, ed. 1960, from Moreau's notebooks (Cahier IV, p. 23).

18 *ibid.*

19 Published in a collection of eleven poems titled *Les Destinées*, 1864. Other poems with similar themes in the same collection were published separately as early as 1843.

20 Marcel Proust, *Contre Sainte-Beuve suivi de Nouveaux Mélanges*, Paris, Gallimard, 1954.

21 Quoted by Deshairs, *op. cit.*

22 Edouard Schuré, *Précurseurs et Révoltés*, Paris, Perrin et Cie., 1904.

23 Note for "Les Filles de Thespius" in cat. Musée G. M., p. 7.

24 Ary Renan, *Gustave Moreau*, ed. 1900.

25 Quoted by Deshairs, *op. cit.*

26 Cat. Musée G. M., p. 11.

27 Cited by Charles Chassé, *Le Mouvement Symboliste*, Paris, 1947, p. 26.

28 Odilon Redon, *A soi-même*, Paris, Floury, 1922, p. 62.

29 Cat. Musée G. M., p. 98.

30 *ibid.*

31 Charles Baudelaire, *L'Art Romantique*, p. 18–19 (cited by H. R. Rookmaaker in *Synthetist Art Theories*, Amsterdam, 1959).

32 Quoted by Roseline Bacou, *Odilon Redon*, Geneva, Cailler, 1956.

33 Mallarmé, *Selected Prose Poems, Essays and Letters*, trans. and intro. by Bradford Cook, Baltimore, Johns Hopkins, 1956, p. 48–49.

34 *ibid.*, p. 100.

35 Charles Baudelaire, *The Mirror of Art*, translated and edited by Jonathan Mayne, New York, Doubleday, 1956, p. 200.

36 J.-K. Huysmans, *op. cit.*, p. 69.

37 J. Alvard, *op. cit.*, p. 43.

38 Alfred H. Barr, Jr., *Matisse: His Art and His Public*, New York, Museum of Modern Art, 1951, p. 36.

39 G. Rouault, *op. cit.*, p. 238.

40 Klaus Brisch, *Wassily Kandinsky* (Dissertation, University of Bonn, 1955, p. 27).

Writing in 1928, Claude Roger-Marx, eloquent champion of Bresdin for half a century, bemoaned the fact that the collection of Bresdin prints in the Cabinet des Estampes in Paris was much inferior to that in the Art Institute of Chicago. This is no longer the case, but the truth remains that, for a long time, the work of the artist was sought after more eagerly in America and Holland than at home. It was in Chicago that the first comprehensive exhibition of his work was held in 1931, with the help of the late J. B. Neumann who has done more than anyone to acquaint wider circles with this immensely rich treasure. Unfortunately, all of this happened nearly half a century after the artist's death. Throughout most of his life he had nursed an image of America as a vast virgin forest where as a colonist he could gain freedom from the bondage of economic worries, and could communicate with a savagely magnificent nature, undefiled by a mercenary civilization. Like many of his contemporaries, he idolized the American Indian and was deeply stirred by the novels of James Fenimore Cooper, particularly *The Last of the Mohicans*, published in 1826 just before the author left America for Paris. He adopted the name of Cooper's hero, Chingachgook, or rather its amusingly corrupted form, Chien-Caillou, as it was pronounced by a half-deaf concierge.

As for the story of Bresdin's life, legend and fantasy appear to be hopelessly entangled with the truth, and a discriminating biography is long overdue. We know that he was born in Ingrande, Loire-Inférieure, in 1822 (earlier sources give Monrelais as his birth place) the son of a metal polisher, and that he went to Paris at the age of twenty. Five years later, he became the hero of Champfleury's *Chien-Caillou*, a morbid but effectively written novel which owed its immediate success to the new vogue for the life of the Bohème whose foremost literary exponent was Murger. Champfleury's description of the young artist's miserable garret—the tiny opening in the ceiling, the crude bed, the ladder on which the live rabbit Petiot is perched above the most rudimentary engraver's tools, and the treasured Rembrandt etching pinned to the wall—is so vivid that no one would question its basic accuracy (even if it were not borne out by other sources). Much less convincing is the story of the sly old Jew, a dealer in second-hand clothing, who bought the starving artist's prints for a pittance and sold them at high prices as the work of an unknown Rembrandt pupil (a designation made by the Cabinet des Estampes, no less). And pure invention is the inevitable sweet and innocent affair with the not so innocent girl Amourette ("I love you even more than my rabbit") who with her sister occupies another room of the attic. But the girls are evicted in the artist's absence, and Chien-Caillou, never finding a trace of them, falls into utter despair resulting in total blindness. (Champfleury could not know it then, but in his later life, Bresdin did suffer from severe eye trouble and came close to being blind). Praised by Victor Hugo, the novel brought fame to Champfleury, but did very little for Bresdin. The Larousse of 1869, in a long chapter on Champfleury, mentions the novel while Bresdin's name appears for the first time in the second supplement of 1890.

After the revolution of 1848, or perhaps only after the coup d'état of 1851, Bresdin left Paris for the far south of France. Alcide Dusolier, in his biographical sketch, *Le Maître au Lapin*, written in 1861, tells that

opposite: Bresdin: *A Clearing in a Forest*. 1880. Etching, 9×6″. The Art Institute of Chicago. The Walter S. Brewster Collection

Bresdin walked all the way from Paris to Toulouse (about 500 miles), carrying the rabbit in his arms. For years, he lived in a rude hut under most primitive conditions. In 1861, he returned to Paris where he had better luck this time. The *Revue Fantaisiste*, which counted Baudelaire, Banville, Alphonse Daudet, Théophile Gautier, and Champfleury among its collaborators, published twelve of his etchings, and in the same periodical, Théodore de Banville wrote a most sympathetic and enthusiastic review of Bresdin's work exhibited at the Salon of 1861, including *The Good Samaritan*. But again, Bresdin felt himself drawn to the South, and as he wanted to be near the sea—still awaiting his chance to go to America—he chose Bordeaux and settled on a little street called Fosse-aux-lions [Lions' Pit], an address which he delighted to put on his prints. It was here that the young Odilon Redon often visited him. By this time, Bresdin had acquired a family: after a liaison that had lasted eight years and produced four children, the long-suffering Rosalie and Bresdin were married in 1865. In 1870, the artist became severely ill with rheumatism and eye trouble, and was hospitalized in Paris, but recovered quickly enough to take part in the uprising of the *Commune* in 1871. We do not know whether it was fear of retribution that made him double his efforts to emigrate, or mere luck: he won a contest to design an American banknote, and gained free passage for himself and his whole family which now comprised six children.

For about a year, while Bresdin supervised the printing of the plate, there seems to have been reasonable prosperity, but then he became again the restless wanderer and took his family to Canada looking for a place in the wilderness to settle down. Soon, the recently earned money was gone, and it was Victor Hugo, always interested in Bresdin, who made it possible for the family to return to France in 1876. For a while Bresdin held a menial job as assistant roadman at the Arc de Triomphe, but his last years he spent in solitude at Sèvres where Champfleury was now Director of the famous porcelain manufactory. In January 1885, Bresdin was found dead in his cold garret room.

Because of the extremely delicate and minute detail, Bresdin's work demands concentrated unhurried study, and above all, a poetic sensibility and mind as attuned to the mysteries of nature as his own. Except for one very small painting, his whole work consists of drawings, etchings and lithographs. Many of his drawings are done with a fine pen in India ink, and though they are generally of small size, their sureness and originality of line are such that they could stand—like the drawings of Callot—any degree of magnification without needing it. A magnificent example of the rich and intricate, yet very pure, polyphony of his penmanship, is the *Crevasse* of 1860. This drawing, like many others, calls to mind the weird and fantastic rock formations of Altdorfer or Roelant Savery and even more of Hercules Seghers, but since it can hardly be assumed that Bresdin had access to their work, this can only be explained by a spiritual affinity.

But he was, to a certain extent, familiar with Rembrandt and possibly also with Dürer. Théodore de Banville, the most penetrating analyst of Bresdin's art, said in the *Revue Fantaisiste* in 1861: "I have mentioned Albrecht Dürer in connection with our artist, but one must not think that Bresdin copied or imitated the great German whose mind gave birth to *Melancholia*, the tearful and savage elegy of a whole century. It is not in the work of the painter of Nuremberg, but in the forest itself where this martyr suffered the agonies of divining the hidden secret, that Bresdin meets Albrecht Dürer ... thus he drained the gall of the same sponge and the ambrosia of the same cup whereby this spy on the living forces of nature became intoxicated."

Much more tangible is the impact of Rembrandt on the early etchings of Bresdin. He tries to adopt the

148

Bresdin: *Studies for The Good Samaritan*. Pen and India ink, 7¹¹/₁₆ × 9″. The Municipal Museum, The Hague

nervous, seemingly chaotic but actually always purposeful manner of Rembrandt, but in the process is apt to become enmeshed in chaos as he did in the wild little etching, *Trees in the Wind*, done at the beginning of his first Paris period. In those days, he also must have become familiar with the etchings of Daubigny from the late thirties and early forties (such as the *Chamois Hunter*) which, in their romantic intensity of feeling, surpass the idyllic, often phlegmatic work of that artist's later years.

His journey to the South, which may have taken him through the spectacular volcanic regions of the Haute Loire or Puy de Dôme, and the solitude of his hut near Toulouse opened up new horizons for him, and his art reached full maturity with *The Holy Family beside a Rushing Stream*, generally assumed to have been done in 1853 though it actually bears the impossible date of 1855. It is one of many versions of the artist's favorite theme, the Flight into Egypt, which runs through his entire work like a leitmotif. Ghostly gnarled trees and the intricate lattice work of naked, weirdly animated branches against a clouded sky set a somber mood which is relieved only by the busy flow of the little stream, a symbol of life and hope in the midst of desolation. Bresdin himself fondly called it *La Vigoreuse*, according to Robert de Montesquiou, who once owned the glorious impression exhibited here, and undoubtedly it is also the print which Redon so warmly admired and rated above *The Good Samaritan*.

149

The *Holy Family* probably was the first lithograph made by Bresdin, and in 1854 it was followed by *The Comedy of Death*, the most macabre of his fantasies. Both these lithographs and many others appear to have been etchings originally and were later transferred upon stones. Bresdin always thought in terms of the pen or the etching needle which is a cousin of the pen, but lithography, to be most effective, calls for the broader and coarser media of crayon or brush. Bresdin ignored that and stuck to his minute method of working with the pen, even on large stones, thereby making the printer's task exceedingly difficult. Again, Banville has most perceptively sensed this when he said that the making of faithful prints from Bresdin's stones would require a master printer, not only of superb competence but of imagination as well, to hold "this black dream-universe where the masses are so large and imposing, burgeoning as nature does with details that are so tiny that a breath can destroy them. And this unheard-of play of light with its infinite scales, with its imperceptible nuances, how can one hope that the lithographic ink will respect it, for it is so accustomed to hiding the mistakes of our artists behind large protective blotches."

The largest and most famous of the lithographs is *The Good Samaritan*, 1861, an incredible tour de force of dedicated attention to minute detail, held together nevertheless by the artist's extraordinary power of imagination which keeps alive every square inch of that immense composition, "the patient and furious work of a genius who desires to embrace everything. . . . In an eternal Hymn, Fauna and Flora are united, where does the animal begin and the vegetation cease?" (Banville). But an even more intimate and touching glorification of the living forest is the etching, *The Forest of Fontainebleau*, surely one of the great prints of the nineteenth century.

Of the many prints done in the Bordeaux period, outstanding are the etchings, *Knight and Death (Le château fort)*, and *The Oriental Rider in a Rocky Landscape*, of 1866. Both, no doubt, made a great impression on the young Redon. In 1868, the lithograph, *Calvary of the Old Caillou* (in a later printing the inscription reads "I have been carrying this Stone for Fifty Years"), poignantly reveals, like an outcry, the artist's tormented state of mind at this time. In a lighter vein are two delightful fantasies, full of animals, people and gingerbread-gothic architecture. *Departure for the Hunt*, and *The Enchanted Castle*, the latter done just prior to his trip to America.

From the beginning of his career, Bresdin had been understood and admired by the great writers and poets of his time, but appears to have been largely ignored by fellow artists and professional art critics. This lot he shared with another great etcher who was but one year older, Charles Meryon. Both were self-taught outsiders, and both won the admiration and support of Victor Hugo and Charles Baudelaire. But Meryon, who had been a sailor in his youth and seen much of the world, did not long for distant virgin forests; the venerable stonework of old Paris was enough to evoke his romantic spirit. There is nothing on record to indicate that the two artists ever met or even knew of each other, both being hermits by nature. Be it accidental or not, they shared certain idiosyncrasies of style, such as a delight in filling their skies with busy little clouds, birds in flight and curled chimney smoke. To be sure, Meryon was not plagued by an overabundance of visions, he was a perfectionist of superb self-control, and though he was the most poetic visual interpreter of the scenery of Paris in the nineteenth century, he always remained a timid draftsman by comparison with Bresdin.

Henri Béraldi, the diligent author of the once leading compendium on the French printmakers of the nineteenth century, writing in 1886, saw in Bresdin an aberration of good taste and an unsound mind. The etchings, of which he only knew a few, he calls "ex-

travagantly bad." Today we see in Bresdin an artist of potent imagination and poetic insight whose technical limitations are an inseparable part of his artistic profile. How could he have been Bresdin if he had commanded the virtuosity of Gustave Doré? His poetry would have been destroyed by it. Artists of our age, groping for new content and new means of expression, feel close to him. The small group of works exhibited here can only serve to incite curiosity about the artist.

There is as yet no serious definitive study of Bresdin's work, nor a completely illustrated descriptive catalogue of his prints. The earliest list of the prints, compiled by Bouvenne, comprises only sixty-one while twice that many are known today. Unfortunately, death has interfered with the completion of the catalogues by Louis Godefroy, J. B. Neumann, and Carl O. Schniewind. A most useful attempt to establish a chronological order has been made by K. G. Boon for an exhibition at the Rijksmuseum in Amsterdam in 1955, and Mr. Boon's numbering has been adopted for our exhibition.

HAROLD JOACHIM

Bresdin: *Bathers in a Mountain Landscape*. (c.1858). Etching, $7^1/_8 \times 9^7/_8''$. The Art Institute of Chicago. The Walter S. Brewster Collection

Bresdin: *The Crevasse*. 1860. Pen and India ink, $8^5/_{16} \times 6^1/_2''$. The Art Institute of Chicago. The Walter S. Brewster Collection

Bresdin: *City in the Mountains*. Pen and India ink, 6¹/₂ × 4⁷/₁₆″. The Art Institute of Chicago. The Walter S. Brewster Collection

Bresdin: *Bank of a Pond*. Pen and India ink, 6⁷/₁₆ × 6¹¹/₁₆″. The Art Institute of Chicago. The Walter S. Brewster Collection

opposite: Bresdin: *The Comedy of Death*. 1854. Lithograph transferred from etching, 8⁹/₁₆ × 5¹³/₁₆″. The Art Institute of Chicago. The Walter S. Brewster Collection

Bresdin: *Forest of Fontainebleau*. Etching, 8 × 5⁷/₈″. The Art Institute of Chicago. The Walter S. Brewster Collection

Bresdin: *Oriental Rider in a Rocky Landscape*. 1866. Etching, 11³/₄ × 9″. The Art Institute of Chicago. The Walter S. Brewster Collection

BRESDIN: DRAWINGS ON STONE, ETCHINGS,
ORIGINAL DRAWINGS

We are sometimes apt to forget the men of merit whom fortune sends us; real talent is not always greeted with the respect it deserves. Wherever thought asserts itself without the support of a militant struggle, without the vigorous contradictions or lively approbations of enthusiasm, it can be said that the man of merit receives inadequate recompense for his generous efforts. That is why, in his own country, the genius often succumbs for lack of adversaries to oppose him or friends to exalt him. Talent coming from afar, already surrounded by the prestige of an established reputation, succeeds no doubt in shining more brightly; but what impediments, what difficulties it still encounters in our unpreparedness, in the inexperience of a few judges who are often too eager to explain it before having completely understood it!

When talent presents itself in a rather free and novel way, our prejudices may at times deceive us, and its finest aspect goes unnoticed by us where it is most worthy and most powerful. M. Bresdin, although much esteemed by a small group of devotees whose admiration is well justified, has not achieved in Bordeaux the position and the recognition which he deserves. His work, although preceded by a justly acquired reputation and already praised by several authoritative critics, has not elicited the excitement which such a fresh and unusual talent seems to demand. None the less, he is truly an artist of refinement: by his great originality, by his rich, varied, and vigorous creation, we rec-

opposite: Bresdin: *The Holy Family with the Does.* 1868. Lithograph, 10³/₈ × 7⁷/₈″. The Art Institute of Chicago. The Walter S. Brewster Collection

Bresdin: *Aqueduct and Waterfalls.* Pen and India ink, 4⁵/₈ × 4³/₄″. Collection Mr. and Mrs. Leonard Baskin, Northampton, Massachusetts ognize the true mark of the artist of high rank and good lineage; for these reasons, above all, he is to be recommended to the attention of art lovers enamored of novel beauties, of rare perfumes, to all those indeed who, bored with insipid imitations, seek art along unknown or unexplored paths.

Three processes serve in turn to express M. Bresdin's unique inspiration: pen drawing on stone, etching, and pen and ink drawing—forming a completely new genre which he alone practices and of which he is, so to speak, the creator. His most widely known work is a large drawing on stone, known by the name of *The Good Samaritan*. A strange creation. We should say here that the artist did not intend to represent the landscape which we see every day from our window; judged from this point of view, this work would certainly be imperfect, for there is no other work among those of our contemporaries which has been less inspired by any spirit of imitation. What he wished, what he attempted, was but to initiate us into the impressions of his own dream. A mystical and very strange dream, it is true, a restless and vague reverie, but what does that matter? Even if the ideal is precise, art, on the contrary, surely draws all its power from its eloquence, its brilliance, its greatness in those things which leave to the imagination the task of defining them.

A conception and the search for the proper elements to formulate it—to strike, to seize our troubled imagination—that is the only theory which governed this work, if indeed the informality of fantasy obeys any law. Considered from this point of view, this work has truly achieved its goal, for no other leaves in our mind such a strong mark, so vivid an impression and one of such great originality.

We can add to this work *The Holy Family*, created by the same process but on a smaller scale, which is much more suitable to this type of drawing where detail is so painstakingly sought. It is more complete, richer, freer in its expression. Nothing could be more naïve, more touching, than this little work, surely created in a moment of auspicious enthusiasm, of abandonment to the ideal. Delicate and careful pursuit of detail, richness of composition—none the less restrained, sober, and simple in effect.

Such is the high aesthetic quality of this work, little known because it is more and more rarely seen, but which will remain certainly as the most complete expression of the strivings of its author. We may also add *The Comedy of Death*, a work of a different scope, less plastic no doubt, but no less interesting. And finally, the drafts for a rather large set of illustrations which the artist was unable to finish. In the first plates of this collection, so special, so different from anything being done today, we can still delve deeply into a real treasure of capricious fantasy.

As an etcher, M. Bresdin is less well known. Nevertheless this versatile and rapid technique is certainly where the artist found his true element. He is acquainted with all its resources and ruses. He was driven to the most subtle and refined efforts by his own temperament, and also by a rigorous conscience, and we can say that his etchings are but a long series of experiments undertaken with the unceasing desire to approach perfection. And what variety, what versatility of means! He attacks the copper with the assurance of an artist for whom the process has ceased to be refractory. We need not insist on that material skill which would make him only a secondary artist, for he possesses a more important merit which gives him a unique place among contemporary etchers: he is a creator.

To all the resources of the subtle and consummate technician he adds the greater qualities of the thinker and the charm of imagination. Indeed, is there anyone more unexpected and more varied in his fantasies? Landscapes, seascapes, battles, interiors, and the most varied of genre subjects serve in turn as an excuse for this vagabond imagination to display here and there its richest caprices and to transform and beautify all the objects which attract it in the wide field it traverses.

The Traveling Tartar Family, the *Old Houses*, etc., are among the pen-and-ink drawings. Here the author is more true to life. This technique, which permits retouching, also allows him to come closer to nature, for which he has always had a humble veneration. We should perhaps point out here the error spread by a few critics who have said too often that M. Bresdin descends too directly from the mystic German masters. Certainly we recognize in him an ardent communion with Rembrandt, and especially with Albrecht Dürer.

Reverence for the masters is not a very great fault, and let us not attach too much blame to archaism. When it is completely understood, archaism is a sanction. A work of art descends directly from another work; if the study of nature gives us the necessary means to manifest our individuality, if observation and patient analysis of reality are the first elements of our language, it is no less true that love of the beautiful, the quest for beautiful models, must incessantly sustain our faith. It is not surprising then if the fervent disciple offers at times the pale image of a god whom he seeks and whom he adores.

Happy indeed are those who feel themselves sufficiently worthy, sufficiently strong, to walk without being dazzled in the light of the glorious masters surrounded by fervent admirers, for whom posterity yet reserves, as an immortal homage, the gift of its finest laurels! Let us welcome their disciples! If M. Bresdin has any relationship to these masters, it must be pointed out that it is much more in this method than in his thought; for his personality has survived durably and victoriously a contact which would have crushed a less gifted disciple. To sustain him he has indeed a vision of the world which no master has taught him.

His distinguishing mark, the thing that no one among the ancients or the moderns could give him, is that unalterable individuality, that remarkable color, which produces throughout his work those strange, mysterious, legendary effects; that freedom with which he handles nature, which reflects, even in the least of his works, an inexpressible sadness. For even though he is awkward in directly reproducing nature, though the poorest student in an academy would be more skillful in representing in detail the objects which meet his eye, the artist is struck by these objects, and often by what is most expressive and most alive in them.

We have certainly seen those bizarre clouds, those murky skies, so profound and so sad. We know what use he has made of those jumbled mixtures full of strange objects, where the eye is led to pursue a thousand and one apparitions. He has also a particular admiration for water in its tender or mysterious aspect. He is, then, a landscape painter; and so, a modern. He always sets his favorite scenes under the open sky; witness *The Traveling Tartar Family*, that work so strongly impregnated with feeling and impression.

Moreover, in a way which is peculiar to the French school, the artist in him is backed up by the thinker. That imagination, impetuous and youthful as it is, seems contained and almost dominated by a constant desire in which the exclusive and dominant state of his interior being is betrayed, though no doubt unconsciously. What we find everywhere, almost from the beginning to the end of his work, is the man enamored of solitude, fleeing desperately under a sky without homeland, in the anguish of a hopeless and unending exile. This dream, this constant anxiety, appears in the most diverse shapes. Sometimes it is in the form of the divine child, in the Flight into Egypt, so often treated by the artist. At times it is a whole family, a legion, an army, a whole people fleeing, always fleeing, from civilized humanity.

This is what especially distinguishes M. Bresdin. This is what the Dutch and German masters could not give him, for this human and philosophical side of art is a quality in which the French school takes pride.

So it is also among the etchings and the original drawings that we must look for the genuine significance of this individuality. It is in these techniques that we must study it in order to succeed in understanding it fully. Therefore, if the City [of Bordeaux] consents to own an example of this artist's work, let it choose from that part which contains his most complete expression, and above all let it put into this choice all the discernment demanded by such a serious undertaking, one so important to true art lovers.

We often believe that people who devote themselves to art are only obeying frivolous taste or inclination; if we look more closely, if our attention becomes more enlightened, we shall see that such at times is the lot of the purest and most severe consciences.

Therefore, if we truly wish to enrich public collections with works worthy of imitation, if we seek these works among artists of merit who contribute new influences to art, we shall always find them among those who, along with the excellence of talent, show that praiseworthy disinterestedness which is always accompanied by sincerity.

These rare natures seldom ask for recognition; their only misfortune is that they retire too easily into a discreetly silent self-communion. Let us go to them; let us try to understand them better by a deeper analysis of their creations. But even though there are still doubts and hesitations concerning the proper appreciation of this artist who has already belonged to Bordeaux for several years, there are none the less a few serious art lovers who did not take long to recognize the true value of this most interesting personality; we believe strongly that their esteem is preparing for him in the future the just approbation which he deserves.

Published in *La Gironde*, January 1st, 1869.
Translated by Alexander and Anne Hull, *The Massachusetts Review*, autumn 1960.

PREFACE FOR THE CATALOGUE OF A BRESDIN RETROSPECTIVE, SALON D'AUTOMNE, PARIS, 1908

Concerning Bresdin, Baudelaire wrote the following letter to Théophile Gautier:

April 29, 1861

My dear Théophile,
You remember my speaking to you of an old friend, M. Rodolphe Bresdin, who has returned here after an absence of twelve years.

I have not heard whether his drawings have been admitted by the Salon jury, but in any case it would be well for you to see some of his work. I know you well enough to sense that there are things that will please you very much. So do welcome Bresdin as an *old* acquaintance; perhaps you will feel that way about him after you have seen his work.

Yours,

BAUDELAIRE

This is how the author of *The Flowers of Evil* wrote of the artist, a group of whose works is now being exhibited; it was evidently high time to show him here among us. The Society of the Salon d'Automne, wishing to do justice and to present without discrimination what is good, cannot better affirm its aims and purpose than by offering to the public—insofar as this is possible for works so scattered and so rare—an exhibition of a little appreciated master who has never had the reputation or recognition he deserves.

The reason for this neglect is that he created an entirely *personal* art. And also that he lived so freely and independently.

Without the sanctions of the academic world of which he was never part, belonging to no group, living—with his impulsive tastes—a life without any plan, having neither formulas nor preconceptions, and especially without feeling either the necessity of belonging to any sect, or of depending on independence, he stood alone. His personality and heart were the

162

gentle and inexorable chemicals which forced the absolute originality of his art to maturity and made it so deserving of praise.

I knew him. The man was a "thoroughbred," fiercely solitary as an artist, jealous of the security given him by the independence of his thought and work to which he surrendered with such passion and fury. He abandoned himself to his instinct. He worked like a child, without discipline, indomitably intolerant of all difficulties.

How could a man of such aristocratic temperament leave his work—cherished, it is true, by faithful admirers, but lost to view for many years—to suffer the fate of those things that are sometimes talked about and then forgotten or never seen at all? It was that fame meant nothing to him. He lived from day to day. With indifference he printed limited editions, sometimes consisting of only three or four proofs, forced by the desire for perfection or the overwhelming necessity of selling in order to satisfy his most immediate needs. As to the works themselves, always strange because of their beauty, never multiplied through large editions, rarely shown by dealers, they were exhibited nowhere. He remained aloof, free, having few friends who were not artists. Finally, there is fate which raises one artist without talent to the height of glory and which does not recognize another, who has created a personal vision, or who reveals the wonders of an undiscovered world to our sensibility. The why of this injustice is a vain question over which the shadow of a mysterious destiny passes in silence.

It was Bresdin's destiny to be exposed to the terrors of poverty. Had he been able to live without family responsibilities—for he was very human, very good—he would have borne hardships with the unassuming pride inseparable from genius and strength of vocation.

His vocation was evident from childhood. Son of a sheet metal worker, predestined to handle copper, as it were, for his mastery was most sure in that medium,

he told me that when he was a youngster he used to pilfer the tools his father had been given for repairs, to make, instinctively, his first attempts at engraving.

As an adolescent he went to Paris, where he was noticed by some writers: Théophile Gautier wrote a poem inspired by his lithograph, *The Comedy of Death*. He knew Champfleury, who gave him reason for complaint. He became acquainted with the engraver Henriquel-Dupont, who showed interest in Bresdin, although he considered him an "original."

In Toulouse, later, he spent some of the most creative years of his obscure career; he told me he left his best works there: pen and ink drawings, etchings, and lithographs which he insisted on calling "drawings on stone."

At the age of about forty-five he moved to Bordeaux, to a street in the suburbs called Fosse-aux-Lions [Lions' Pit], where I saw him every day. With a kind of sad humor he detected in the name of that street something of his destiny and sometimes, wryly, inscribed the address on his prints. Thickset and powerful in build, he had short arms; his hands were beautiful. I can still remember his troubled face, a little surly, but with clear, animated eyes. I see him bent over by the window, anxiously following the progress of the acid biting into the copper, or else, bending over the small drawings on bristol paper which he drew with such careful concentration and of which, when they were sold, he always kept a tracing done rapidly, a beautiful tracing enriched by the addition of new inventions.

His power lay in imagination alone. He never conceived anything beforehand. He improvised with joy, completing with tenacity the entanglements of the barely perceptible vegetation of the forests he dreamt up, which you see now before you. He adored nature. He spoke about it softly, tenderly, with a voice that suddenly became convincing and solemn, thus contrasting with the usually whimsical and playful tone

163

of his conversation. "My drawings are real, whatever one may say!" he frequently affirmed.

It is certain that in his work people considered fantastic that which is human, though emerging mysteriously from a distant atavism. Born in Brittany, Bresdin saw as a child those old Breton houses, rivers, and woods. He was moved by the melancholy skies. He dreamt of virgin forests and went to Canada when he was well on in years. But he returned disappointed —his dream had been more beautiful than reality.

The master he worshipped above all others was Rembrandt, who overwhelmed him. He called him his God. Only Rembrandt and a constant love of nature inspired him.

I am not going to try to explain his work because what is beautiful cannot be explained. His art is the result of a precarious existence, martyred and full of suffering, disillusioned and broken by the hazards of fate. Understand the spirit of his work, see in these minute surfaces the expression of an ingenious, genial naïveté, of a distant, humble, confused, and sorrowful humanity. But behind this appearance, which is not unlike that of old German prints, there still lies a good deal of French inventiveness. And yet, nothing of this master is owned by our museums. The lithograph of the Samaritan was shown in 1900 at the Centennial exhibition, but the beautiful drawings and etchings did not accompany it.

Such rare works should appeal to collectors. The most unexpected and unhoped-for group was assembled by the artist's daughter, Rodolphine, who—childishly attracted by images—secretly gathered precious proofs. With pride and dignity she also maintained the cult of her father, whom I loved so much. I have a debt to this artist; the respect he had for the subtle resources of the stone captivated me; he taught me to evolve continuously through a love for the masters and through one's own means.

EXCERPTS FROM NOTES FOR A LECTURE DELIVERED IN HOLLAND, JANUARY 1913

... Rodolphe Bresdin initiated me, with the greatest respect for my own independence, into the art of engraving and lithography. He did not practise the latter on paper, nor did he draw with lithographic crayon. This visionary, whose eyes and heart were openly fixed on the world of appearance, worked only with a pen and produced by stippling the most minute elements proper to the expression of his dream. Besides admirable etchings, he has left some lithographs whose blacks are very solid. He fashioned them with perpetual concern for the lithographic ink. He diluted it gravely, quietly, precisely; observing him, one felt how this initial operation, of so little importance to others, was in some way decisive for him. He treated the liquid with consideration and care, protecting it from the deadly presence of dust which might have ruined his efforts. His meticulous precautions reminded me of the Dutch master who, for similar reasons, moved his studio to the cellar where no one but he could penetrate and to which he would descend softly and slowly, so as not to raise any noxious atoms capable of disturbing the purity of his oils and pigments.

Even though he was French, Bresdin, born near the Loire river, had in his tastes and his life something of the old masters, fond of beautiful textures. He was poor and surrounded by precarious objects, but anything he touched with his fine hands gave one the feeling of something rare and precious. When he worked, his long, thin fingers seemed even further elongated, as if fluids linked them to his tools. They were not the hands of a prelate; they were conscious, loving, sensitive to substances, they did not disdain humble objects, yet they were refined and elegant, soft and supple as an aristocrat's. The hands of an artist. They revealed, as did his whole person, a being different from others, with a fatal destiny, a being predestined to suffer heavily and sadly from the daily shocks of ordinary life. The artist, that accident, that person for whom there is nothing in the social world except the love and admiration of the few with whom he has affinities, is condemned to submit to hardship and disenchantment when he is born without fortune. But Bresdin, with an innate gift for cheerfulness and vitality, carried these wounds proudly; to those who could see, his exterior showed goodness. . . .

He gardened with pleasure and with the minute care of a Chinese. Subtle and meticulous in everything, he carried his fineness, his delicacy, his curiosity for analysis and observation to his garden. It was then, more than at any other time, that he was alert and overflowed with sudden and surprising words which left me thoughtful. Once he said to me in a voice of gentle authority: "Do you see this chimney flue? What does it tell you? To me it tells a story. If you have the energy to observe it well and to understand it, then you will imagine the strangest and most bizarre subject. If this subject is based on—and remains within the limits of—this simple face of a wall, your dream will be alive. There is art." Bresdin said this in 1864. I specify the date because this was not then the method of teaching.

Today I am happy to have heard, in my youth, a very original artist whom I loved and admired say these somewhat subversive things which I understood so well and which confirmed what I myself vaguely felt. In an apparently simple form, they give the principles of an elevated education. They open the painter's eyes to the two aspects of life, the two realities it is impossible to separate without lessening art and depriving it of the noble and supreme things it can give.

The artists of my generation, for the most part, have looked at a chimney flue and have seen only a chimney flue. That which the reflection of our own essence can add to a blank wall they were not able to provide. Anything that exists in the beyond, that illuminates and amplifies the object and raises the spirit into the region of mystery, into the troubled atmosphere of the irresolute and its delicious worries was absolutely closed to them. Anything that lent itself to symbolism, all the elements of the unexpected, the imprecise, the undefinable which art contains and which give it an aspect bordering on the enigmatic, they avoided; it frightened them. True parasites of the object, they have cultivated art on a purely visual plane and have closed it, so to speak, to anything beyond this which might have been capable of endowing even the humblest essays, even black and white images, with spiritual light. I mean the irradiation which envelops our spirit—and which escapes all analysis.

One might be seized with regret when confronted with these undeniable gaps, were it not for the memory of all that which flowered everywhere during my youth. Those who have seen, as I have, the course which artistic creation took in that epoch, will understand that the artists with closed minds of whom I speak had, alas!, their reason for being and to what extent they obeyed, consciously or not, a law of necessary rejuvenation and refreshment. Through his pupils, the influence of David was at its apogee: confined production, dry, incapable of abandon, derived from abstract formulas, when it would have been sufficient to open one's eyes to the magnificence of nature in order to liberate and revitalize it.

Everything considered, we should be grateful, therefore, to those of my contemporaries [the impressionists] who took the good road, the road of truth, of nature. Even though their trees are not always high, their skies are low, and the clouds too heavy to attract our dreams, some of these artists have nevertheless walked, resolute and manly, along their road, with the daring of rebels convinced for an instant that they were holding at least a part of truth. If the edifice they built does not offer profound perspectives, the air is pure there just the same, and one can breathe.

Bresdin did not understand their struggle because he was of another time; he was of 1822. The small village in which he was born had placed only peaceful and rustic pictures before his young eyes. He did not want to do them better; he loved them. He told me that when he was a little boy scrawling and engraving on copper, the curé, surprised by his endeavors, became his first patron. Oh! the good curé who added a love for art to the austere exercise of his vocation. Even tolerating some emancipation, he enlightened Bresdin's parents to the calling of their child and advised them to let him go elsewhere, to a better environment, and follow a future different from the one to which they destined him. For his father was a tanner.

In what region, in what social world did the precious dispositions of the child arise, which were to blossom later in the rare flower of originality? One might suppose that Bresdin thought of the good curé who had pointed out the divine star to him, when he subsequently etched the touching images of the Flight into Egypt, a subject he loved and of which he created so many variations. Did he not himself always travel in imagination towards better worlds? He drew families traveling, barbarians immigrating, armies, legions, or tribes in flight. I would not insist on the abundance and variety of his works if they were not so little known, if proofs were not so rare and small in number.

I believe he told me that his mother was of nobility, and this explains perhaps the disparate traits of his character. He was of the masses and yet an aristocrat. Without doubt he retained from this origin the peculiarities of his strange nature: fantastic, childish, abrupt and kind, suddenly withdrawn, suddenly open and cheerful. The natural truth of his utterances was in itself rich with good advice, to be gathered without the strain of a solemn education. With him everything took on a flippant form in order to make you think, often even with a smile. This was real humor. He did not understand nor did he like academic art. It upset him that a certain master [Ingres] should have spoken of "probity" in regard to drawing. "Color is life itself," he said. "It annihilates the line with its rays." And one felt that his convictions on this point were his very own, that they derived from his cult for natural, instinctive invention.

Alas! how what I heard him say contrasted with what was taught in the art schools! What lessons did we receive, even those who came after me? Is it possible for the teacher, as he makes his round in the studio among the students grouped in front of the model, is it possible for him to tell each the basic truth, to speak the fertile word, the one that will bring forth in each his own particular law? No, hardly. In every pupil, in every child is there not a surprising mystery of what is to come? And will the teacher have the tact, the perspicacity, and the insight to transform the first stammerings of his pupil into fertile flowerings?

After all, the one who teaches wants to continue the action of the masters, but—alas!—lacks their sanction even to transmit it. He vests himself with it as best he can through the analysis of the beautiful works of the past, consecrated by time, but—like a grammarian—he only gains from them an abstract experience, mere formulas, devoid of the authority provided by love. Yet one must love in order to believe, and one must believe in order to act; the one who instructs best is the one who has already touched the student with a kind of creative revelation that stems from the beauty of his own work. . . .

With Bresdin one did not forget either the cult of nature or the cult of the masters, particularly Rembrandt, whom he adored. "Rembrandt," he said, "painted only beggars, cripples, old people, but what nobility, what depth, what poetry; there was something of God in him!"

I liked to attribute to this fervent disciple something of the master he adored. Like him, he lived in humble suburbs among poor people who evidently mistrusted his appearance and bearing. He was mysterious, not by disdain, but by natural superiority, so as to maintain—unsoiled and active—the interior resources of his own life. The masses do not understand that relationship. They admit it only in circumstances other than those of an artist whose sufferings they do not even guess. They are ignorant of the frictions which promiscuity produces when it meets with refinement of culture. The artist, however, without mingling with the masses, will always love their spontaneity because it nourishes his vision of that which is natural and because he finds there, more than in mundane spheres, the innate generosity of gestures and passions.

I saw him live in Bordeaux in extreme poverty, which through his intensive labors he managed to forget. His street ... was near the beautiful cemetery of the Chartreuse which I sometimes crossed when I went to see him, very early in the morning. It was in the spring. This season in Bordeaux has a delicious softness; the atmosphere is humid and hot under a clear sky, the light is limpid. I do not know whether it is the passage of time which amplifies the impressions of youth, but nowhere else have I ever tasted so strongly the invigorating charm of my walks along the solitary little streets with narrow sidewalks leading to his home. These were half built, unpopulated sections where trees rose from gardens behind low walls or palisades, and where the fallen hawthorn blossoms on the road plunged me into strange dreams as I trampled them.

At that time of the year, especially when one is young, with what freshness do our sensitive fibers not vibrate! And how the stimuli change: I would not walk on flowers today. It would seem to me that I were committing a profanation, that I was mutilating grossly, even though they had fallen and their short life was spent, those fragile, perfumed beings, adorable prodigies of light. I used to crush them with voluptuous pleasure for the strange shiver I felt and the even stranger course my thoughts took in the act. It was like a confused memory of things that had happened before my own birth, the echo of gentle joys, of happy enchantments. And this contrasted with the habitual state of my mentality, then so morose and melancholy. In the same notebook in which I gathered the pronouncements of my old friend Bresdin, which I jotted down secretly—as I also hid from him my own notes— I find these lines scrawled with a sickish handwriting, which I give you as the forerunners of my own blacks and shadows (lines which I would no longer write today): "I have passed through the cold and silent paths of the cemetery, by deserted tombs. And I have known calmness of spirit. Oh death, how great you are: in the calm your thought gives me, how you strengthen me against care!" ...

Published in O. Redon: *A soi-même*, Paris, 1922, 1961.

BIBLIOGRAPHIES

REDON: BIBLIOGRAPHY *by John Rewald*

For additional documentation see bibl. 20, 25, 55, 59, 63. Bibl. 58 contains 158 classified and annotated references.

1 REDON, ODILON. Salon de 1868. *La Gironde* May 19, June 9, July 1, 1868.

2 HENNEQUIN, EMILE. Odilon Redon. *Revue Littéraire et Artistique* Mar. 4, 1882.

3 HUYSMANS, JORIS-KARL. L'Art moderne. Paris, 1883.

4 HUYSMANS, JORIS-KARL. A Rebours. Paris, 1884.

5 MORICE, CHARLES. Odilon Redon. *Les Hommes d'Aujourd'hui* v. 8, no. 386, 1890.

6 SYMONS, ARTHUR. A French Blake. *Art Review* (London) July 1890.

7 GAUGUIN, PAUL. Huysmans et Redon [written 1890–91]. See bibl. 54.

8 RODHE, JOHAN. Journal fra en Rejse i 1892. [Copenhagen, 1955].

9 AURIER, ALBERT. Les Symbolistes. *Revue Encyclopédique* Apr. 1892.
   Reprinted in his "Oeuvres posthumes." Paris, 1893.

10 BERNARD, EMILE. Odilon Redon. *Le Coeur* Sept.–Oct. 1893.

11 MAUCLAIR, CAMILLE. Exposition Odilon Redon. *Mercure de France* May 1, 1894.

12 REDON, ODILON. Letter to E. Picard (June 15, 1894). *Nieuwe Rotterdamsche Courant* Jul. 4, 1894.
   Also in *L'Art Moderne* Aug. 25, 1894.

13 DENIS, MAURICE. Odilon Redon. *L'Art et la Vie* Oct. 1896.

14 DENIS, MAURICE. Exposition Odilon Redon. *L'Occident* Apr. 1903.
   Nos. 13 and 14 reprinted in Denis' "Théories (1890–1910)." Paris, 1912.

15 BERNARD, EMILE. Odilon Redon. *L'Occident* May 1904.

16 REDON, ODILON. Rodolphe Bresdin *in* Salon d'Automne. [Catalogue of Bresdin Retrospective]. Paris, 1908.

17 REDON, ODILON. Confidences d'artiste. [written 1909].

La Vie Nov. 30, 1912; Nov., Dec. 1916.
   Reprinted in his "A soi-même." Paris, 1922, 1961.

18 HOMMAGE À ODILON REDON. *La Vie* Nov. 30, Dec. 7, 1912.
   Contributions by Bonnard, Denis, Mellerio, Sérusier, van Dongen, Valtat, etc.

19 PACH, WALTER. Odilon Redon. New York, 1913.
   Published in connection with the Armory Show.

20 MELLERIO, ANDRÉ. L'Oeuvre graphique complet d'Odilon Redon. Paris, 1913.
   Bibliography. For larger reproductions of lithographs see: Odilon Redon – Oeuvre graphique complet. 2 v. The Hague [1913]. Supersedes DESTRÉE, JULES. L'Oeuvre lithographique d'Odilon Redon. Brussels, 1891.

21 DOIN, JEANNE. Odilon Redon. *Mercure de France* July 1, 1914.

22 SÉRUSIER, PAUL. Odilon Redon. *La Vie* May 15, 1920.

23 REDON, ODILON. À Soi-Même – Journal (1867–1915). Paris, 1922, 1961.
   "Notes sur la vie, l'art et les artistes."

24 REDON, ODILON. Lettres d'Odilon Redon, 1878–1916, publiées par sa famille. Paris & Brussels, 1923.

25 MELLERIO, ANDRÉ. Odilon Redon. Peintre, Dessinateur et Graveur. Paris, 1923.
   Catalogue; bibliography.

26 PACH, WALTER. The Masters of Modern Art. New York, 1924.

27 HERTZ, HENRI. Odilon Redon. *Art in America* Oct. 1924.

28 ROGER-MARX, CLAUDE. Odilon Redon. Paris, 1925.

29 Recueil de Lettres à Emile Bernard. Tonnerre, 1926. New edition, Brussels, 1942.

30 ROGER-MARX, CLAUDE. Odilon Redon. *Burlington Magazine* June 1926.

31 MAUS, OCTAVE. Trente Années de Lutte pour l'Art, 1884–1914. Brussels, 1926.

32 MIEDEMA, R. Odilon Redon en Albrecht Dürer. Amsterdam, 1928.

33 CHICAGO. ART INSTITUTE. Odilon Redon: Paintings, Pastels and Drawings. 1928.
   Catalogue of exhibition, Dec. 1928–Jan. 1929.

34 FEGDAL, CHARLES. Odilon Redon. Paris, 1929.

35 BORN, WOLFGANG. Der Traum in der Graphik des Odilon Redon. *Graphische Kunst*, 1929.

36 NEW YORK. MUSEUM OF MODERN ART. Toulouse-Lautrec, Odilon Redon. 1931.
   Catalogue of exhibition held Jan. 31–Mar. 2.

37 AURIANT. Des lettres inédites d'Odilon Redon. *Beaux-Arts* June 7, 1935; Redon et Emile Hennequin. *Beaux-Arts* June 14, 1935.

38 MORLAND, JACQUES. Odilon Redon et le Symbolisme. *Mercure de France* Aug. 1, 1936.

39 PACH, WALTER. Queer Thing, Painting: Forty Years in the World of Art. New York, 1938.

40 MESURET, ROBERT. La maison natale d'Odilon Redon. *La Renaissance* Mar. 8, 1939.

41 LEBLOND, MARIUS-ARY. Les Fusains d'Odilon Redon. Paris, 1941.

42 EDWARDS, HUGH. Redon, Flaubert, Vollard: drawings for "The Temptation of Saint Anthony." *Art Institute of Chicago Bulletin* Jan. 1942.

43 DORIVAL, BERNARD. Les Etapes de la Peinture française contemporaine. v. 1. Paris, 1943.

44 JOHNSON, UNA E. Ambroise Vollard, Editeur, 1867–1939. New York, 1944.

45 CHASSÉ, CHARLES. Le Mouvement Symboliste dans l'Art du XIXe Siècle. Paris, 1947.

46 SEZNEC, JEAN. The Temptation of Saint Anthony in Art. *Magazine of Art* Mar. 1947.

47 NATANSON, THADÉE. Peints à leur Tour. Paris, 1948.

48 SEZNEC, JEAN. Nouvelles Études sur la Tentation de St. Antoine. London, 1949.

49 OOSTING, J. B. Odilon Redon. *Maandblad voor beeldende Kunsten* July 1949.

50 ROGER-MARX, CLAUDE. Redon – Fusains. Paris, 1950.

51 PARIS. MUSÉE DE L'ORANGERIE. Eugène Carrière et le Symbolisme. 1949.
   Exhibition catalogue, Dec. 1949–Jan. 1950. Bibliography.

52 SELIGMANN, JACQUES, & COMPANY. Odilon Redon: Pastels and Drawings. New York, 1961.
   Catalogue of exhibition also shown at Cleveland Museum and Walker Art Center, Nov. 1951–Feb. 1952.

53 NEW YORK. MUSEUM OF MODERN ART. Redon: Drawings and Lithographs. – Picasso: His Graphic Art. 1952.
   Exhibition catalogue, also issued as Bulletin, v. 19, no. 2. Text by W. S. Lieberman.

54 LOIZE, JEAN. Un inédit de Gauguin. *Nouvelles Littéraires* May 7, 1953.
   Includes bibl. 7.

55 SANDSTRÖM, SVEN. Le Monde imaginaire d'Odilon Redon. Lund, 1955.
   Comprehensive bibliography.

56 SOCIETY OF THE FOUR ARTS, PALM BEACH, FLORIDA. Odilon Redon. 1955.
   Catalogue of exhibition held Mar.–Apr.

57 WASHINGTON, D. C. CORCORAN GALLERY OF ART. Visionaries and Dreamers. 1955.
   Catalogue of exhibition held Apr.–May. Text by Henri Dorra.

58 REWALD JOHN. Post-Impressionism – From van Gogh to Gauguin. New York, 1956.
   Bibliography, p. 579–583.

59 BACOU, ROSELINE. Odilon Redon. 2 v. Geneva, 1956.
   Extensive documentation in v. 2.

60 REDON, ARÏ. Odilon Redon dans l'intimité. *Revue des Arts* Oct. 1956.

61 LEBLOND, MARIUS-ARY. J'ai vu Odilon Redon face à face avec Rembrandt. *Arts* Oct. 24–30, 1956; Mon ami Mallarmé par Odilon Redon. *Arts* Oct. 31–Nov. 6, 1956; Odilon Redon et Francis Jammes. *Arts* Nov. 14–20, 1956.

62 REWALD, JOHN. Quelques notes et documents sur Odilon Redon. *Gazette des Beaux-Arts* Nov. 1956.

63 PARIS. MUSÉE DE L'ORANGERIE. Odilon Redon. 1956.
   Bibliography. Exhibition held Oct. 1956–Jan. 1957.

64 BERGER, KLAUS. The Pastels of Odilon Redon. *College Art Journal* Fall, 1956.

65 THE HAGUE. GEMEENTEMUSEUM. Odilon Redon. 1957.
   Exhibition catalogue, May–June.

66 MASSON, ANDRÉ. Redon: Mystic with a Method. *Art News* June 1957.

67 LEBLOND, MARIUS-ARY. Redon et l'impressionnisme. *Le Peintre* Oct. 1, 1957.

68 JACQUINOT, J. Huysmans et Odilon Redon. *Bulletin de la Société J.-K. Huysmans* no. 33, 1957.

69 BERGER, KLAUS. The Reconversion of Odilon Redon: Reflections on an Exhibition. *Art Quarterly* Summer 1958.

70 HIGGINS, STEPHEN, GALERIE. Odilon Redon: Magicien du noir et blanc. Paris, 1958.
   Catalogue of exhibition, June–Sept.

71 BERNE. KUNSTHALLE. Odilon Redon. 1958.
   Exhibition catalogue, Aug.–Oct.

72 NEW GALLERY. Odilon Redon. New York, 1958.
   Exhibition catalogue, Nov.

73 ROSENBERG, PAUL & Co. Paintings and Pastels by Odilon Redon. New York, 1959.
   Catalogue of exhibition, Feb. 9–Mar. 7.

74 MATTHIESEN GALLERY. Odilon Redon, 1840–1916. London, 1959.
   Catalogue of exhibition held May–June.

75 HOMAGE TO REDON. Northampton, Mass., Gehenna Press, 1959.
   "Ten portraits cut & engraved on wood by George Lockwood, with Redon's Essay on Bresdin, lithography and the nature of black translated by H. Swetzoff." From text written in 1913.

76 REDON, ARÏ, ed. Lettres de Gauguin, Huysmans, Jammes, Mallarmé, Verhaeren . . . à Odilon Redon. Paris, 1960.
   Texts and notes by R. Bacou.

77 REWALD, JOHN. The History of Impressionism. 3rd rev. ed. New York, 1961.

MOREAU: BIBLIOGRAPHY *by Dore Ashton*

1 BACOU, ROSELINE. Odilon Redon. 2 v. Geneva, 1956.

2 BÉNÉDITE, LÉONCE. Gustave Moreau et Burne-Jones. Paris, 1922.

3 BEURDELEY, CÉCILE. Gustave Moreau. *Connaissance des Arts* no. 45: 38–43 Nov. 15, 1955.

4 BOUYER, RAYMOND. Le don de Charles Hayem. *Gazette des Beaux-Arts* 24: 593–598 1900.

5 BRETON, ANDRÉ. L'Art Magique. Paris, 1957.

6 CASTAGNARY, JULES-ANTOINE. Salons (1857–1870). v. 1. Paris, 1892.

7 CHARENSOL, GEORGES. Gustave Moreau. *L'Art Vivant* 2 no. 31: 252–254 Apr. 1, 1926.

8 CHASSÉ, CHARLES. Le Mouvement Symboliste dans l'Art du XIXe Siècle. Paris, 1947.

9 CHESNAU, ERNEST. L'Education de l'Artiste. Paris, 1880.
   Translated by Clara Bell (New York, London, 1886).

10 COQUIOT, GUSTAVE. Des gloires déboulonnées. Paris, 1924.

11 DESHAIRS, LÉON and LARAN, JEAN. Gustave Moreau. Paris, 1913.

12 DESVALLIÈRES, GEORGES. L'Oeuvre de Gustave Moreau. Paris, 1913.

13 DIMIER, LOUIS. L'inspiration de Gustave Moreau. *Minerva* (Paris) 1 no. 18: 261–279 Nov. 15, 1902.

14 DORIVAL, BERNARD. Les Etapes de la Peinture française contemporaine. 3 v. Paris, 1943–1946.

15 EVÈNEPOEL, HENRI. Gustave Moreau et ses Elèves. Paris, 1923.

16 FELS, FLORENT. L'Art Vivant. Geneva, 1950.

17 GEFFROY, GUSTAVE. L'Oeuvre de Gustave Moreau. Paris, 1900.

18 HAUTECOEUR, LOUIS. Littérature et Peinture en France, du XVIIe au XXe Siècle. Paris, 1942.

19 HOLTEN, RAGNAR VON. L'Art Fantastique de Gustave Moreau. Paris, 1960.

20 HUNEKER, JAMES GIBBONS. Promenades of an Impressionist. New York, 1910.

21 HUYSMANS, JORIS-KARL. A Rebours. Paris, 1884.

22 JEAN, MARCEL. Histoire de la Peinture Surréaliste. Paris, 1959.
   Translated by S. W. Taylor: New York, 1960.

23 LARROUMET, GUSTAVE. Notice Historique sur la Vie et les Oeuvres de M. Gustave Moreau. Paris, 1901.

24 LEPRIEUR, PAUL. Gustave Moreau et son Oeuvre. Paris, 1889.

25 MAUCLAIR, CAMILLE. De Watteau à Whistler. Paris, 1905.

26 PARIS, MUSÉE DU LOUVRE. Gustave Moreau. 1961.
   Exhibition catalogue; introduction by J. Cassou and J. Paladilhe, notes by R. von Holten.

27 PARIS. MUSÉE GUSTAVE MOREAU. Catalogue Sommaire des Peintures, Dessins, Cartons et Aquarelles Exposés dans les Galeries du Musée Gustave Moreau. Paris, 1904.
   Catalogue by Paul Flat. New edition, Paris, 1926.

28 PETIT, GEORGES, GALERIE. Gustave Moreau. Paris, 1906.
   Catalogue; text by Robert de Montesquiou.

29 PROUST, MARCEL. Contre Sainte-Beuve, suivi de Nouveaux Mélanges. Paris, 1954.

30 REDON, ODILON. A Soi-Même: Journal 1867–1915. Paris, 1922, 1961.

31 RENAN, ARY. Gustave Moreau. Paris, 1900.

32 REWALD, JOHN. The History of Impressionism. 3rd rev. ed. New York, 1961.

33 REWALD, JOHN. Post-Impressionism – From van Gogh to Gauguin. New York, 1956.

34 ROUAULT, Souvenirs Intimes. Paris, 1927.
   Text on Moreau previously published as a special issue of L'Art et les Artistes, April 1926.

35 SCHURÉ, EDOUARD. Précurseurs et Révoltés. Paris, 1904. Also in 1920 edition.

36 The Splendrous Art of Gustave Moreau, Life, July 21, 1961.

37 THÉVENIN, LÉON. L'Esthétique de Gustave Moreau. Paris, 1897.

38 VAUCAIRE, MICHEL. Salomé à travers l'art et la littérature. Nouvelle Revue (Paris) 46: 145–151 May 15, 1907.

39 WASHINGTON, D.C. CORCORAN GALLERY OF ART. Visionaries and Dreamers. 1955.
   Catalogue of exhibition, Apr.–May. Text by Henri Dorra.

BRESDIN: BIBLIOGRAPHY   by Harold Joachim

1 CHAMPFLEURY (pseud. of JULES FLEURY). Chien-Caillou. Paris, 1847.
   Novel also published 1860, and in 1906 by Floury, with preface by Henri Boutet.

2 DUSOLIER, ALCIDE. Le Maître au Lapin. 1861.

3 BANVILLE, THÉODORE DE. Le Salon de 1861. Revue Fantaisiste (Paris) 2:164–173 June 15, 1861.

4 FOURÈS, AUGUSTE. Rodolphe Bresdin dit Chien-Caillou. Carcassonne, 1891.
   "Avec fac-similé de dessins originaux et dix lettres inédites."

5 FAGE, ÉMILE. Chien-Caillou. Bulletin, Société des Lettres, Sciences et Arts de la Corrèze (Tulle) 19:157–183 1897.

6 PARIS. SALON D'AUTOMNE. 6e Exposition. Oct.–Nov. 1908.
   Includes: Odilon Redon. Rodolphe Bresdin, 1822–1885. Préface pour l'exposition rétrospective d'oeuvres de Bresdin, organisée par J. Perrichon.

7 MONTESQUIOU-FEZENSAC, ROBERT DE. L'Inextricable Graveur, Rodolphe Bresdin. Paris, 1913.

8 BOUVENNE, AGLAÜS. Catalogue de l'oeuvre de Bresdin dit Chien-Caillou. L'Amateur d'Estampes 1 no. 5:4 Apr. 25, 1922; no. 7: 6–8 June 25, 1922.
   Part I: Eaux-fortes, – II: Lithographies.

9 REY, ROBERT. Rodolphe Bresdin. L'Amour de l'Art 5 no. 10:327–333 Oct. 1924.

10 ROGER-MARX, CLAUDE. Rodolphe Bresdin, called "Chien-Caillou." Print Collector's Quarterly 14 no. 3: 251–270 July 1927.

11 ROGER-MARX, CLAUDE. Rodolphe Bresdin, dit Chien-Caillou. L'Amour de l'Art 9 no. 4:137–141 Apr. 1938.

12 NEUMANN, J.B., ed. Rodolphe Bresdin. New York, Artlover Library, 1929.
   Catalogue with 110 illustrations of his etchings and lithographs in v. 1 of "The Artlover Library"; additional illustrations in v. 2: Living Art, and v. 3: European Art.

13 KNUTTEL, G.W. Rodolphe Bresdin. Mededeelingen van den Dienst vor Kunsten en Wetenschappen der Gemeente s'Gravenhage 2 no. 7: 206–18 Nov. 1930.

14 CHICAGO. ART INSTITUTE. Exhibition of Etchings, Lithographs and Drawings by Rodolphe Bresdin. Chicago, 1931.

15 AMSTERDAM. RIJKSMUSEUM. Rodolphe Bresdin: Etsen en Lithografiëen. Amsterdam, 1955.
   Preface by I. Q. van Regteren Altena; introduction and catalogue by K. G. Boon.

16 ROGER-MARX, CLAUDE. Bresdin l'étrange. L'Oeil (Paris) no. 5:5–11 May 15, 1955.

17 HOMAGE TO REDON. Northampton, Mass., Gehenna Press, 1959.
   Includes "Redon's essay on Bresdin, lithography and the nature of black" (written 1913).

18 RODOLPHE BRESDIN, 1822–1885. Massachusetts Review 2 no. 1: 73–100 Autumn 1960.
   Translations of: "Bresdin l'étrange" by Claude Roger-Marx, "Odilon Redon on his master Bresdin" from A soi-même, "Bresdin in America" as told by his daughter to Marius-Ary Leblond. – "Paul Bresdin on his father." Letter by Baudelaire; list of sources. Also issued in reprint dedicated to J. B. Neumann.

LENDERS TO THE EXHIBITION

Jere Abbott, Dexter, Maine; Mr. and Mrs. James W. Alsdorf, Winnetka, Illinois; Mr. and Mrs. Leonard Baskin, Northampton, Massachusetts; Mrs. Richard J. Bernhard, New York; Mrs. A. Bonger, Almen, The Netherlands; Dr. and Mrs. B. K. Boom, Amsterdam, The Netherlands; Henri Dorra, Philadelphia; Jacques Dubourg, Paris; Richard L. Feigen, Chicago; Allan Frumkin, Chicago; Mr. and Mrs. Matthew H. Futter, New York; Mr. and Mrs. Charles Goldman, New York; Dr. Hans R. Hahnloser, Bern; Huntington Hartford, New York; Mr. and Mrs. H. Lawrence Herring, New York; Stephen Higgons, Paris; Mrs. H. Harris Jonas, New York; Mr. and Mrs. E. Powis Jones, New York; Mr. and Mrs. Werner E. Josten, New York; Dr. R. A. Kling, New York; Mrs. Albert D. Lasker, New York; Robert Lebel, Paris; Mrs. Arthur Lehman, New York; Mr. and Mrs. Robert Lehman, New York; Dr. and Mrs. Theodore Leshner, Brooklyn; Mr. and Mrs. Isadore Levin, Detroit; Mr. and Mrs. Alex M. Lewyt, New York; Charles K. Lock, New York; Louis Macmillan, New York; Dr. J. E. van der Meulen, The Hague; Mrs. Nikifora Pach, New York; Mr. and Mrs. Lazarus Phillips, Montreal; Peter Andrews Putnam, Cleveland; Arï Redon, Paris; Mr. and Mrs. David Rockefeller, New York; Mrs. John D. Rockefeller, 3rd, New York; Mrs. Sam Salz, New York; Mr. and Mrs. Norbert Schimmel, Kingspoint, New York; Mr. and Mrs. Irving W. Schwartz, New York; Mrs. Mabel Garrison Siemonn, New York; Mr. and Mrs. Sidney Simon, New City, New York; Mrs. Charles E. Slatkin, New York; Mrs. Bertram Smith, New York; Louis E. Stern, New York; Mr. and Mrs. Donald S. Stralem, New York; Mr. and Mrs. Donald B. Straus, New York; Mr. and Mrs. Harold X. Weinstein, Chicago; The Honorable and Mrs. John Hay Whitney, New York; Georges Wildenstein; Ian Woodner, New York.

George A. Lucas Collection, The Maryland Institute (on permanent loan to The Baltimore Museum of Art); The Art Institute of Chicago; The Dallas Museum of Fine Arts; The Detroit Institute of Arts; Municipal Museum, The Hague; Wadsworth Atheneum, Hartford; Yale University Art Gallery, New Haven; The Metropolitan Museum of Art, New York; The Museum of Modern Art, New York; Rijksmuseum Kröller-Müller, Otterlo; Musée Gustave Moreau, Paris; Musée du Louvre, Paris; Musée du Petit Palais, Paris; The Art Museum, Princeton University, Princeton; City Art Museum of St. Louis; The Phillips Collection, Washington, D. C.

Findlay Galleries, Inc., Chicago; Stephen Hahn Gallery, New York; The New Gallery, New York; Paul Rosenberg & Co., New York; E. and A. Silberman Galleries, New York.

Dates enclosed in parentheses do not appear on the paintings. In dimensions, height precedes width. Works marked with an asterisk are illustrated.

REDON: PAINTINGS AND PASTELS

* 1 *Arab Horsemen.* (c. 1865). Oil on canvas, $11^1/_2 \times 10''$. Collection Mrs. Nikifora Pach, New York. Ill. p. 51

* 2 *Self Portrait.* (1867). Oil on wood, $16^1/_8 \times 12^5/_8''$. Collection Arï Redon, Paris. Ill. p. 18

* 3 *The Distributor of Laurel Wreaths.* (Before 1870). Oil on paper applied to cradled panel, $16^1/_2 \times 19^5/_8''$. Collection Stephen Higgons, Paris. Ill. p. 16

  4 *Trees at Peyrelebade.* (c. 1875). Oil on paper mounted on canvas, $9^1/_2 \times 13''$. Collection The Honorable and Mrs. John Hay Whitney, New York

* 5 *Landscape, Peyrelebade.* (c. 1880). Oil on cardboard, $18^1/_8 \times 17^3/_8''$. Collection Arï Redon, Paris. Ill. p. 52

* 6 *Street in Quimper, Brittany.* (c. 1880). Oil on cardboard, $12^3/_8 \times 9''$. Collection Arı Redon, Paris. Ill. p. 30

  7 *Sailboat in Brittany.* (c. 1880). Oil on cardboard, $8^1/_8 \times 12^3/_8''$. Collection Arï Redon, Paris

* 8 *Near the Harbor, Brittany.* (c. 1880). Oil on canvas, $7^1/_2 \times 10^3/_4''$. Collection Mrs. Richard J. Bernhard, New York. Ill. p. 54

  9 *Countryside at Peyrelebade.* (c. 1880). Oil on board, $13 \times 10''$. Stephen Hahn Gallery, New York

*10 *Portrait of Mme Redon.* 1882. Oil on canvas, $17^3/_4 \times 14^1/_2''$. Musée du Louvre, Paris. Ill. p. 55

*11 *Symbolic Head.* (1890). Oil on canvas, $21 \times 15^1/_4''$. Collection Mr. Peter Andrews Putnam, Cleveland. Ill. p. 63

 12 *The Virgin of Dawn.* (1890). Oil on paper, $20^5/_8 \times 15''$. Collection Mr. and Mrs. Isadore Levin, Detroit

*13 *Fallen Angel.* (1890–1905). Oil on canvas, $31^7/_8 \times 39^3/_8''$. E. and A. Silberman Galleries, New York. Ill. p. 65

 14 *Allegory.* (c. 1895). Oil on canvas, $20 \times 14''$. Collection Mrs. Mabel Garrison Siemonn, New York

*15 *Head with Flowers.* (c. 1895). Oil on canvas, $20^1/_2 \times 18^1/_2''$. Collection Mrs. Arthur Lehman, New York. Ill. p. 67

 16 *Hippocampes.* (1896). Pastel, $19 \times 19''$. The New Gallery, New York

 17 *Portrait of Arï in Profile.* (1896–97). Oil on cardboard, $16^1/_8 \times 8^1/_4''$. Collection Arï Redon, Paris

*18 *Arï Redon.* (1897). Pastel, $17^7/_8 \times 12^3/_8''$. The Art Institute of Chicago. Gift of Kate L. Brewster. Ill. p. 77 (Shown in Chicago only)

*19 *Cyclops.* (c. 1898). Oil on wood, $25^1/_4 \times 20''$. Rijksmuseum Kröller-Müller, Otterlo. Ill. p. 64

*20 *The Doge's Wife.* (c. 1900). Oil on canvas, $25 \times 14^3/_4''$. Paul Rosenberg & Co., New York. Ill. p. 69

*21 *The Fall of Phaeton.* (c. 1900). Oil on canvas, $28^3/_4 \times 21^1/_4''$. Collection Mr. and Mrs. Werner E. Josten, New York. Ill. p. 78

 22 *Dream Shadows.* (c. 1900). Pastel, $18^3/_4 \times 24''$. Collection Mr. and Mrs. Sidney Simon, New City, New York. (Shown in New York only)

 23 *St. Sebastian.* (c. 1900). Pastel, $26^1/_4 \times 21''$. Collection Mr. and Mrs. Norbert Schimmel, Kingspoint, New York. (Shown in New York only)

 24 *Gothic Window.* (1900). Oil on canvas, $25^1/_4 \times 19^3/_4''$. Collection Mr. and Mrs. Lazarus Phillips, Montreal

 25 *Sea Monster.* (c. 1900). Pastel, $21 \times 15''$. Findlay Galleries, Inc., Chicago. (Shown in Chicago only)

*26 *Etruscan Vase.* (1900–05). Tempera on canvas, $31^3/_4 \times 23''$. The Metropolitan Museum of Art, New York. The Maria DeWitt Jessup Fund, 1951. Ill. p. 70

 27 *Pomegranate on a Plate.* (1901). Oil on canvas, $9^5/_8 \times 9^5/_8''$. Collection Dr. R. A. Kling, New York

*28 *Five decorative panels.* (1902). Oil and gouache on canvas, $8' \ 4^5/_8'' \times 6' \ 1^3/_4''$, $8' \ 4^3/_8'' \times 2' \ 8^3/_4''$, $8' \ 4^1/_2'' \times 2' \ 6^1/_2''$, $8' \ 4^1/_4'' \times 1' \ 4^1/_2''$, $8' \ 4^5/_8'' \times 1' \ 1/_4''$. Private collection, Charlotte, Vermont. Originally executed for Mme Ernest Chausson. One ill. p. 41

29 *Flight into Egypt.* (1902). Pastel and gouache, 19³/₄ × 24″. Collection Mrs. John D. Rockefeller, 3rd, New York. (Shown in New York only)

30 *Woman with Pillar of Flowers.* (1903). Pastel, 23 × 19″. Collection Dr. and Mrs. Theodore Leshner, Brooklyn

*31 *Woman with Flowers.* (1903). Pastel, 26 × 19³/₄″. Collection Mrs. H. Harris Jonas, New York. (Shown in New York only). Ill. p. 68

*32 *Eve.* (1904). Oil on canvas, 24 × 18¹/₈″. Collection Jacques Dubourg, Paris. Ill. p. 74

33 *Andromeda.* (c. 1905). Oil on canvas, 21 × 20¹/₄″. The Art Institute of Chicago. The Mr. and Mrs. Martin A. Ryerson Collection

*34 *At the Bottom of the Sea.* (c. 1905). Oil on canvas, 23 × 19″. Collection Mr. and Mrs. Charles Goldman, New York. Ill. p. 76

35 *Evocation.* (c. 1905). Pastel, 20¹/₂ × 14¹/₄″. The Art Institute of Chicago, The Joseph Winterbotham Collection. (Shown in Chicago only)

36 *Flowers in a Vase.* (c. 1905). Oil on canvas, 25³/₄ × 19³/₄″. Collection Mr. and Mrs. Donald S. Stralem, New York

*37 *Jacob Wrestling with the Angel.* (c. 1905). Oil on wood, 18¹/₂ × 16¹/₄″. Collection Mr. and Mrs. Matthew H. Futter, New York. Ill. p. 82

*38 *Two Heads among Flowers.* (c. 1905). Oil on canvas, 24 × 19³/₄″. Private collection, Cambridge, Massachusetts. Ill. p. 71

39 *The Sailboat.* (1905). Oil on canvas, 13 × 16¹/₄″. Private collection, New York

*40 *Ophelia.* (1905–06). Oil on board, 22⁷/₈ × 18¹/₈″. Collection Ian Woodner, New York. Ill. p. 72

*41 *The Green Death.* (After 1905). Oil on canvas, 21⁵/₈ × 18¹/₂″. Collection Mrs. Bertram Smith, New York. Ill. p. 75

*42 *Still Life: Vase of Flowers.* (c. 1910). Oil on cardboard, 27 × 21″. The Art Institute of Chicago. The Mr. and Mrs. Lewis L. Coburn Memorial Collection. Ill. p. 81

43 *Mystery.* (c. 1910). Oil on canvas, 29 × 21¹/₂″. The Phillips Collection, Washington, D.C.

*44 *The White Butterfly.* (c. 1910). Oil on canvas, 25 × 19¹/₄″. Collection Ian Woodner, New York. Ill. p. 84

*45 *Pandora.* (c. 1910). Oil on canvas, 56¹/₂ × 24¹/₂″. The Metropolitan Museum of Art, New York. Bequest of Alexander Max Bing, 1959. Ill. p. 88

46 *Apollo.* (c. 1910). Oil on canvas, 26 × 32″. The Metropolitan Museum of Art, New York. Anonymous gift, 1927

*47 *Flowers in a Green Vase.* (c. 1910). Oil on canvas, 21¹/₂ × 29¹/₄″. Collection The Honorable and Mrs. John Hay Whitney, New York. Ill. p. 86

*48 *Ophelia.* (c. 1910). Pastel, 25 × 36″. Collection Mrs. Albert D. Lasker, New York. Originally an upright representation of a vase of flowers standing on a base, this pastel was later turned horizontally by the artist, and the head of Ophelia added to it. Ill. p. 80

*49 *Phaeton.* (c. 1910). Oil on canvas, 21 × 8¹/₄″. Collection Mr. and Mrs. Sidney Simon, New City, New York. Ill. p. 79

*50 *Roger and Angelica.* (c. 1910). Pastel on paper on canvas, 36¹/₂ × 28³/₄″. The Museum of Modern Art, New York. The Lillie P. Bliss Collection. (Shown in New York only). Ill. p. 85

51 *Butterflies.* (c. 1910). Oil on canvas, 21³/₄ × 16¹/₄″. The Detroit Institute of Arts

*52 *Animals of the Sea.* (1910). Oil on canvas, 14 × 9¹/₂″. Collection Mr. and Mrs. Irving W. Schwartz, New York. Ill. p. 87

*53 *Apparition.* (1910). Oil on canvas, 25⁷/₈ × 20″. The Art Museum, Princeton University, Princeton. Ill. p. 83

*54 *Silence.* (c. 1911). Oil on linen-finish paper, 21¹/₄ × 21¹/₂″. The Museum of Modern Art, New York. The Lillie P. Bliss Collection. Ill. p. 93

*55 *Birth of Venus.* (c. 1912). Oil on canvas, 55¹/₂ × 24″. Collection Stephen Higgons, Paris. Ill. p. 88

56 *Young Woman.* (c. 1912). Pastel, 25 × 19″. The Art Institute of Chicago. The Mr. and Mrs. Martin A. Ryerson Collection. (Shown in Chicago only)

*57 *Sea Anemones.* (c. 1912). Oil on canvas, 20 × 17″. The New Gallery, New York. Ill. p. 91

*58 *Andromeda.* (1912). Oil on canvas, 69 × 36″. Collection Mr. and Mrs. David Rockefeller, New York. Ill. p. 89

*59 *Head of a Woman in a Shell.* (1912). Oil on cardboard, $21^3/_8 \times 21^1/_4''$. Collection Dr. Hans R. Hahnloser, Bern. Ill. p. 73

*60 *Vase of Flowers with Butterflies*. (1912–14). Oil on canvas, $28^3/_4 \times 21^1/_4''$. Private collection, Dallas, Texas, through the courtesy of The Dallas Museum of Fine Arts. Ill. p. 92

61 *Vase of Flowers*. (c. 1914). Pastel, $28^3/_4 \times 21^1/_8''$. The Museum of Modern Art, New York. Gift of William S. Paley. (Shown in New York only)

62 *Yellow Flowers*. (1914). Pastel, $25^1/_2 \times 19^1/_2''$. The Museum of Modern Art, New York. Acquired through the Mary Flexner Bequest. (Shown in New York only)

REDON: WATERCOLORS

63 *Study of a Head with Flowers*. (c. 1910–12). Watercolor, $10^5/_8 \times 8^1/_4''$. Cabinet des Dessins du Musée du Louvre, Paris

64 *The Horse*. (c. 1910–12). Watercolor, $9^3/_4 \times 7''$. Collection Dr. Hans R. Hahnloser, Bern

65 *Face in a Shell*. (c. 1910). Watercolor, $6^1/_4 \times 8^5/_8''$. Collection Louis Macmillan, New York

66 *The Red Scarf*. (c. 1910). Watercolor, $9^1/_2 \times 6^1/_2''$. Collection Mrs. Sam Salz, New York

67 *Fantasy*. (c. 1910). Watercolor, $7^1/_4 \times 10''$. E. and A. Silberman Galleries, New York

*68 *Butterflies and Sea Horses*. (1910–14). Watercolor, $6 \times 9^1/_8''$. Private collection, New York. Ill. p. 45

69 *Butterflies*. (1910–14). Watercolor, $10^1/_4 \times 8^1/_4$. Collection Louis E. Stern, New York

70 *Woman with Arms Outstretched*. (1910–14). Watercolor, $6^3/_4 \times 8''$. Musée du Petit Palais, Paris. Donation Jacques Zoubaloff

71 *Butterfly and Flowers*. (1910–14). Watercolor, $8^7/_8 \times 6^3/_4''$. Musée du Petit Palais, Paris. Donation Jacques Zoubaloff

*72 *Butterflies and Plants*. (1910–14). Watercolor, $6^3/_4 \times 9^1/_4''$. Musée du Petit Palais, Paris. Donation Jacques Zoubaloff. Ill. p. 45

73 *Profile of a Woman*. (c. 1912). Watercolor, $7^3/_4 \times 6^1/_4''$. Collection Arï Redon, Paris

*74 *Fish (Souvenir of a Visit to the Aquarium of Ar-* *cachon*. (1912). Watercolor, $11 \times 8^5/_8''$. Collection Mr. and Mrs. Alex M. Lewyt, New York. Ill. p. 90

REDON: DRAWINGS

*75 *Roland at Roncevaux*. (c. 1865). Pen and ink, $13^3/_8 \times 10^1/_4''$. Collection Charles K. Lock, New York. Ill. p. 50

*76 *Two Figures in a Mountain Landscape*. (c. 1865). Pen and India ink wash on bristol board, $9^7/_8 \times 6^5/_8''$. Musée du Petit Palais, Paris. Donation Jacques Zoubaloff. Ill. p. 51

77 *Warrior on Horseback*. (c. 1865). Pencil, pen, brush and ink on tan paper, $12^3/_4 \times 18^1/_8''$. Rijksmuseum Kröller-Müller, Otterlo

78 *Dante and Virgil*. (1865). Charcoal on brown paper, $9^3/_8 \times 14^1/_2''$. Collection Mrs. A. Bonger, Almen, The Netherlands

79 *Dante and Virgil in a Landscape*. (1865–70). Charcoal, $12^1/_2 \times 9^3/_4''$. The New Gallery, New York

80 *Sunset*. (1865–70). Charcoal, $9^7/_8 \times 16^3/_4''$. Collection Allan Frumkin, Chicago

*81 *Basement at Peyrelebade*. (c. 1870). Pencil, $9^1/_2 \times 8^1/_2''$. Collection Arï Redon, Paris. Ill. p. 22

82 *Portrait of a Young Man*. (c. 1870). Pencil on pink paper, $5^1/_2 \times 5^1/_2''$. Collection Arï Redon, Paris

*83 *Apparition*. (1870–75?). Pencil on brown paper, $7^3/_4 \times 7^1/_2''$. Collection Mrs. Charles E. Slatkin, New York. Ill. p. 53

*84 *Stone*. (1870–75). Pencil, $5 \times 11''$. Collection Arï Redon, Paris. Ill. p. 22

85 Copy after Leonardo da Vinci's *The Virgin and St. Anne* [Musée du Louvre]. (c. 1875). Charcoal, $9^1/_4 \times 10^1/_2''$. Collection Arï Redon, Paris

86 *Man in a Large Hat*. (c. 1875). Pencil, $4^3/_4 \times 4^1/_8''$. Cabinet des Dessins du Musée du Louvre, Paris

87 *The Tree*. (c. 1875). Pencil, $8 \times 5^5/_8''$. Collection Arï Redon, Paris

*88 *Winged Head above the Waters*. (c. 1875). Charcoal on tan paper, $18^1/_4 \times 14^5/_8''$. The Art Institute of Chicago. The David Adler Collection. Ill. p. 56

89 *The Duenna*. (1875–80). Charcoal on tan paper, $12^5/_8 \times 11''$. Collection Stephen Higgons, Paris

*90 *Eyes in the Forest.* (1875–80). Charcoal on brown paper, $13^1/4 \times 10^3/4''$. City Art Museum of St. Louis. Ill. p. 58

*91 *Head of an Old Woman.* (1875–80). Charcoal on brown paper, $14^3/8 \times 11^5/8''$. Rijksmuseum Kröller-Müller, Otterlo. Ill. p. 10

92 *The Sorceress.* (1879). Charcoal on tan paper, $16 \times 14^5/8''$. The Art Institute of Chicago. The David Adler Collection

*93 *Cyclops.* (c. 1880). Pencil, $4^5/8 \times 6^1/4''$. Private collection, New York. Ill. p. 28

94 *The Horse.* (c. 1880). Pencil, $7 \times 5^5/8''$. Collection Arï Redon, Paris

95 *The Prisoner.* (c. 1880). Charcoal, $14^1/8 \times 20^1/8''$. Collection Mr. and Mrs. E. Powis Jones, New York

96 *The Tree Dweller.* (c. 1880). Charcoal on tan paper, $18^5/8 \times 13^1/4''$. The Art Institute of Chicago. The David Adler Collection

*97 *The Weeping Spider.* (c. 1880). Charcoal on brown paper, $19^1/2 \times 14^3/4''$. Collection Dr. and Mrs. B. K. Boom, Amsterdam. Ill. p. 57

98 *Young Girl at the Window.* (c. 1880). Pencil, $10^3/8 \times 7^1/2''$. Collection Arï Redon, Paris

99 *Sketchbook.* (One page dated 1880). Pencil, $7^3/8 \times 4^3/8''$. The Art Institute of Chicago. The William McCallin McKee Memorial Collection

*100 *The Cactus Man.* (1881). Charcoal on beige paper, $18^1/4 \times 12^3/8''$. Collection Ian Woodner, New York. Ill. p. 59

101 *The Eye like a Strange Balloon Moves towards Infinity.* (1882). Charcoal, $16^7/8 \times 13''$. The Museum of Modern Art, New York. Gift of Larry Aldrich

*102 *Mask of the Red Death.* (1883). Charcoal, $16^1/2 \times 14^1/8''$. The New Gallery, New York. Ill. p. 62

103 *Dream Polyp.* (c. 1885). Charcoal, $18^3/4 \times 14''$. Collection Mr. and Mrs. Donald B. Strauss, New York

*104 *Figure in Armor.* (c. 1885). Charcoal, $19^7/8 \times 15''$. The Metropolitan Museum of Art, New York. The Dick Fund, 1948. Ill. p. 60

105 Interpretation of Rembrandt's *Susanna and the Elders.* (c. 1885). Pencil, $10^3/4 \times 9^1/2''$. Collection Arï Redon, Paris

106 *Hamlet.* (c. 1885). Pencil, $5^1/2 \times 5''$. Collection Arï Redon, Paris

*107 *A Flower with a Child's Face.* (c. 1885). Charcoal on tan paper, $15^7/8 \times 13''$. The Art Institute of Chicago. The David Adler Collection. Ill. p. 61

*108 *Marsh Flower.* (c. 1885). Charcoal on brown paper, $16^3/4 \times 14''$. Collection Mr. and Mrs. H. Lawrence Herring, New York. Ill. p. 61

109 *Skeleton in the Woods.* (c. 1885). Charcoal on tan paper, $18^3/4 \times 12^1/4''$. Collection Mr. and Mrs. James W. Alsdorf, Winnetka, Illinois

110 *Shrouded Woman.* (c. 1885). Charcoal on tan paper, $20^1/4 \times 14^3/4''$. The Art Institute of Chicago. The David Adler Collection

*111 *Germination.* (1885). Charcoal, $20^1/2 \times 15''$. Collection Henri Dorra, Philadelphia. Ill. p. 59

112 *Portrait of Mme Redon.* (1885). Charcoal on tan paper, $15^1/4 \times 12^1/2''$. Collection Arï Redon, Paris

113 *Portrait of Vuillard.* (Before 1886?). Pen and ink, $10^7/8 \times 9''$. Collection Mrs. Nikifora Pach, New York. Redon presented this drawing to the late Walter Pach and supposedly told him that it represented Vuillard; it has been repeatedly exhibited and reproduced with this designation. However, it seems possible that there exists a confusion between Vuillard and "Vieillard" (old man). Indeed, this drawing appears to be a study for the lithograph *A la Vieillesse* (M. 62), done in 1886, for which Mellerio mentions the existence of a preparatory drawing. This drawing may actually be the work catalogued as *Vieillard* in the Armory Show, No. 284 (although no medium is specified). Redon did execute a lithographic portrait of Vuillard, dated 1900; however this does not seem as closely related to the present drawing as the lithograph of 1886, which is *not* a likeness of the Nabis painter, who was then eighteen years old.

114 *The Accused.* (1886). Conté crayon on gray paper, $21 \times 14^5/8''$. The Museum of Modern Art. Acquired through the Lillie P. Bliss Bequest

115 *Pegasus and Bellerophon.* (c. 1890). Charcoal, $21^1/8 \times 14^1/8''$. Collection Mr. and Mrs. Robert Lehman, New York

116 *Owl.* (c. 1890?). Pencil, $10 \times 7^1/4''$. Private collection, New York.

117 *Young Girl.* (c. 1890). Conté crayon on tan paper, $19^3/4 \times 14^1/4''$. The Museum of Modern Art, New York. Gift of John S. Newberry

118 *Eclosion.* (c. 1890). Charcoal on tan paper, 19⁷/₈ × 14⁷/₈″. The Art Institute of Chicago. The David Adler Collection

*119 *Tree.* (c. 1892). Pencil, 18 × 12¹/₄″. Collection Jere Abbott, Dexter, Maine. Ill. p. 27

*120 *Self Portrait.* (c. 1895?). Crayon, 13³/₈ × 8⁷/₈″. Collection Dr. J. E. van der Meulen, The Hague. Ill. p. 66

121 *Profile.* (c. 1895). Charcoal on tan paper, 20³/₄ × 14⁷/₈″. The Art Institute of Chicago. The David Adler Collection

122 *Silhouette of a Young Woman.* (c. 1895). Charcoal on tan paper, 18¹/₂ × 13⁷/₈″. The Art Institute of Chicago. The David Adler Collection

123 *Crucifixion.* (1895–98). Charcoal on tan paper, 19³/₈ × 13³/₈″. Yale University Art Gallery, New Haven. Everett V. Meeks Fund

124 *Portrait of the Artist's Son.* (1898). Pencil, 11 × 6″. Collection Arï Redon, Paris

*125 *Chimera.* (1902). Charcoal on brown paper, 21⁵/₈ × 15¹/₄″. Collection Mrs. A. Bonger, Almen, The Netherlands. Ill. p. 25

126 *Seated Nude.* (1904). Sanguine on gray paper, 19¹/₂ × 13⁵/₈″. Collection Mr. and Mrs. Alex M. Lewyt, New York

127 *Mysterious Medallion.* (c. 1910). Brush and ink, 5³/₄ × 3³/₄″. Collection Arï Redon, Paris

128 *Man with Arms Crossed.* (c. 1910). Brush and ink, 6 × 4¹/₂″. Collection Arï Redon, Paris

129 *Nudes.* (1910–12). Pen, brush, and ink, 9 × 7″. Musée du Petit Palais, Paris. Donation Jacques Zoubaloff

REDON: PRINTS

Unless otherwise indicated, these prints are in the collection of The Art Institute of Chicago, The Stickney Fund. Through this fund the personal print collection of the artist was purchased from his widow in 1920.

The initial "M" followed by a number refers to the catalogue established by A. Mellerio: *L'oeuvre graphique complet d'Odilon Redon*, Paris, 1913.

Etchings

130 *The Ford.* (c. 1865). 6⁷/₈ × 5⁵/₁₆″ (composition). (M. 2)

131 *Battling Horsemen.* (1865). 4 × 7¹³/₁₆″ (plate). (M. 4)

*132 *Fear.* (c. 1865). 5¹/₂ × 8¹³/₁₆″ (plate). (M. 6). Ill. p. 97

133 *Two Trees.* 1865. 4³/₈ × 7⁷/₈″ (plate). (Unknown to Mellerio)

134 a. *Galloping Horseman.* (1866). 3 × 5³/₄″ (plate). (M. 10)
   b. *Apparition.* The composition has been reworked with a drypoint needle. (State unknown to Mellerio)

*135 *Tobias.* (c. 1880). 7⁷/₈ × 5³/₄″ (plate). (M. 15)
   a. First state. Ill. p. 96
   b. Second state
   c. Third state

136 *Cain and Abel.* (1886). Etching and drypoint, 7⁵/₁₆ × 4³/₄″ (plate). (M. 18)

Lithographs

All lithographs listed here as in the collection of The Museum of Modern Art, New York, except number 167, will be replaced in Chicago by impressions belonging to The Art Institute of Chicago, The Stickney Fund.

*137 *Eclosion,* Plate I from *Dans le rêve,* 1879. 13¹/₈ × 10¹/₄″. (M. 27). Ill. p. 99

*138 *The Eye like a Strange Balloon Moves towards Infinity,* Plate I from *À Edgar Poe,* 1882. 10³/₈ × 7³/₄″. (M. 38). The Museum of Modern Art, New York. Gift of Peter H. Deitsch. Ill. p. 98

*139 *The Breath that Impels Beings Is also in the Spheres,* Plate V from *À Edgar Poë,* 1882. 10¹¹/₁₆ × 8³/₁₆″. (M. 42). Ill. p. 98

*140 *The Deformed Polyp Floats on the Strand, a Kind of Smiling and Hideous Cyclops,* Plate III from *Les origines,* 1883. 8⁷/₁₆ × 7¹³/₁₆″. (M. 47). The Museum of Modern Art, New York. Gift of Victor S. Riesenfeld. Ill. p. 28

*141 *The Swamp Flower, a Sad and Human Face,* Plate II from *Hommage à Goya,* 1885. 10¹³/₁₆ × 8″. (M. 55). The Museum of Modern Art, New York. Mrs. John D. Rockefeller, Jr., Purchase Fund. Ill. p. 101

142 *Awakening I Saw the Goddess of the Intelligible with a Profile Austere and Obdurate,* Plate VI from *Hommage à Goya,* 1885. 10¹/₂ × 8¹/₂″. (M. 59). The Museum of Modern Art, New York. Mrs. John D. Rockefeller, Jr., Purchase Fund

143 *The Egg.* (1886). 11¹/₂ × 8⁷/₈″. (M. 60). The Museum of Modern Art, New York. Gift of Peter H. Deitsch

144 *Profile of Light.* (1886). 13³/₈ × 9¹/₂″. (M. 61)

*145 *To Old Age,* Plate I from *La nuit,* 1886. 9¹/₄ × 7¹/₄″. (M. 62). Ill. p. 100

146 *Surrounded by Night the Man Was Alone,* Plate II from *La nuit,* 1886. 11⁹/₁₆ × 8⁵/₈″. (M. 63). The Museum of Modern Art, New York. Gift of Mrs. John D. Rockefeller, Jr.

*147 *Christ.* (1887). 12⁷/₈ × 10⁷/₈″. (M. 71). Ill. p. 102

*148 *The Spider.* (1887). 11 × 8¹/₂″. (M. 72). The Museum of Modern Art, New York. Mrs. Bertram Smith Fund. Ill. p. 103

*149 *A Skull was Revealed by the Gap in the Wall,* Plate IV from *Le juré,* 1887. 9³/₈ × 7¹/₄″. (M. 78). An early state unknown to Mellerio, before the reduction of the composition. Ill. p. 104

150 *Is There Not an Invisible World . . . ,* Plate V from *Le juré,* 1887. 8⁵/₈ × 6³/₄″. (M. 79). The Museum of Modern Art, New York. Purchase Fund

*151 *Death: "Mine Irony Surpasseth all Others,"* Plate III from *À Gustave Flaubert,* the second series of the *Tentation de Saint-Antoine,* 1889. 10¹/₄ × 7³/₄″. (M. 97). Ill. p. 34

*152 *Pegasus Captive.* (1889). 13³/₈ × 11⁵/₈″. (M. 102, the second state). The Museum of Modern Art, New York. The Lillie P. Bliss Collection. Ill. p. 105

153 *The Serpent Crowned with a Halo.* (1890). 11⁷/₈ × 8⁷/₈″. (M. 108). The Museum of Modern Art, New York. Purchase Fund

*154 *And Below Was the Astral Idol, the Apotheosis,* Plate II from *Songes,* 1891. 10⁷/₈ × 7¹/₂″. (M. 111). The Museum of Modern Art, New York. Given anonymously. Ill. p. 104

*155 *The Light of Day,* Plate VI from *Songes,* 1891. 8¹/₄ × 6¹/₈″. (M. 115). The Museum of Modern Art, New York. The Lillie P. Bliss Collection. Ill. p. 106

*156 *The Reader* (believed to be an idealized portrait of Bresdin). (1892). 12¹/₄ × 9⁵/₁₆″. (M. 119). The Museum of Modern Art, New York. Gift of Mrs. John D. Rockefeller, Jr. Ill. p. 94

*157 *Tree.* (1892). 18³/₄ × 12⁵/₈″. (M. 120). The Museum of Modern Art, New York. Gift of Mrs. John D. Rockefeller, Jr. Ill. p. 27

158 *Light.* (1893). 15⁷/₁₆ × 10³/₄″. (M. 123). The Museum of Modern Art, New York. Gift of Victor S. Riesenfeld

159 *Obsession.* (1894). 14¹/₄ × 9″. (M. 128)
    a. First state
    b. Second state. The Museum of Modern Art, New York. Gift in Memory of Bertha M. Slattery

160 *Brünnehilde.* (1894). 11¹/₂ × 14³/₄″. (M. 130)

161 *I Buried Myself in Solitude and I Lived in the Tree Behind Me,* Plate IX from *Tentation de Saint-Antoine,* the third series, 1896. 11³/₄ × 8⁷/₈″. The Museum of Modern Art, New York. Gift of Mrs. John D. Rockefeller, Jr.

162 *. . . And Single Eyes Floated like Mollusks,* Plate XIII from *Tentation de Saint-Antoine,* the third series, 1896. 12¹/₈ × 8⁷/₈″. (M. 146). The Museum of Modern Art, New York. Gift of Mrs. John D. Rockefeller, Jr.

*163 *Anthony: "What Is the Object of all this?"/The Devil: "There is no Object."* Plate XVIII from *Tentation de Saint-Antoine,* the third series, 1896. 12³/₈ × 9⁷/₈″. (M. 151). The Museum of Modern Art, New York. Gift of Mrs. John D. Rockefeller, Jr. Ill. p. 107

164 *Like Spirit Forms I Have Sometimes Seen in the Sky . . . ,* Plate XXI from *Tentation de Saint-Antoine,* the third series, 1896. 10³/₈ × 7³/₈″. (M. 151). The Museum of Modern Art, New York. Gift of Mrs. John D. Rockefeller, Jr.

165 *The Beasts of the Sea, Swollen like Wine Skins,* Plate XXII from *Tentation de Saint-Antoine,* the third series, 1896. 10³/₈ × 7⁵/₈″. (M. 154). The Museum of Modern Art, New York. Gift of Mrs. John D. Rockefeller, Jr.

166 *The Shulamite.* (1897). Printed in color. 9³/₄ × 7⁵/₈″. (M. 167)

167 *Beatrice.* (1897). Printed in color. 13¹/₈ × 11¹/₂″. (M. 168). The Museum of Modern Art, New York. Gift of Mrs. John D. Rockefeller, Jr.

168 *Arï.* (1898). Printed in sanguine. 7³/₄ × 5″. (M. 170, state not described). The Museum of Modern Art, New York. Mrs. Bertram Smith Fund

169 *. . . And Behold a Pale Horse; And His Name That Sat on Him Was Death,* Plate III from *Apocalypse de Saint-Jean,* 1899. 12³/₈ × 8⁷/₈″. (M. 176). The

Museum of Modern Art, New York. Gift of Mrs. John D. Rockefeller, Jr.

170 *And to Him Was Given the Key of the Bottomless Pit*, Plate VIII from *Apocalypse de Saint-Jean*, 1899. $12 \times 9^{1}/_{8}''$. (M. 181)

171 *Pierre Bonnard*. (1902). $5^{5}/_{8} \times 4^{3}/_{4}''$. (M. 191). The Museum of Modern Art, New York. Larry Aldrich Fund

*172 *Paul Sérusier*. 1903. $6^{3}/_{8} \times 5^{1}/_{4}''$. (M. 192). Ill. p. 36

Book

173 Edmond Picard: *Le juré*, Monodrame en cinq actes; sept interprétations originales (lithographs) par Odilon Redon, Brussels, 1887. The Art Institute of Chicago

MOREAU: PAINTINGS

*174 *Cavalier*. (c. 1855). Oil on canvas, $18^{1}/_{4} \times 15^{1}/_{8}''$. Musée Gustave Moreau, Paris. Ill. p. 111

*175 *Oedipus and the Sphinx*. 1864. Oil on canvas, $81^{1}/_{8} \times 41^{1}/_{4}''$. The Metropolitan Museum of Art, New York. Bequest of William H. Herriman, 1921. Ill. p. 113

*176 *Thomyris and Cyrus*. Oil on canvas, $23^{5}/_{8} \times 35^{3}/_{8}''$. Musée Gustave Moreau, Paris. Ill. p. 128

*177 *Salome Dancing before Herod*. (c. 1870). Oil on canvas, $55^{1}/_{2} \times 41''$. Collection Huntington Hartford, New York. Ill. p. 116

*178 *Hercules and the Hydra of Lerne*. (c. 1876). Oil on canvas, $70^{3}/_{4} \times 60^{3}/_{4}''$. Collection Richard L. Feigen, Chicago. Ill. p. 117

*179 *Galatea*. Oil and gouache on canvas, $14^{5}/_{8} \times 10^{3}/_{8}''$. Collection Mr. and Mrs. Harold X. Weinstein, Chicago. Ill. p. 136

*180 *Galatea*. (c. 1880). Oil on wood, $33^{3}/_{8} \times 26^{3}/_{8}''$. Collection Robert Lebel, Paris. Ill. p. 136

181 *St. Sebastian*. Oil on wood, $9^{5}/_{8} \times 12^{5}/_{8}''$. Collection Stephen Higgons, Paris

*182 *St. Cecilia*. Oil on canvas, $33^{7}/_{8} \times 26^{3}/_{4}''$. Musée Gustave Moreau, Paris. Composition cut below and probably repainted at a later date. Ill. p. 119

183 *The Good Samaritan*. Oil on canvas, $32^{1}/_{4} \times 39^{3}/_{8}''$. Musée Gustave Moreau, Paris

*184 *Delilah*. Oil on canvas, $12^{1}/_{8} \times 15^{3}/_{4}''$. Musée Gustave Moreau, Paris. Ill. p. 121

*185 *Circe*. Oil on canvas, $18^{1}/_{8} \times 15^{1}/_{4}''$. Musée Gustave Moreau, Paris. Ill. p. 129

*186 *Orpheus at the Tomb of Eurydice*. Oil on canvas, $68^{1}/_{2} \times 50^{3}/_{8}''$. Musée Gustave Moreau, Paris. Ill. p. 125

*187 *The Apparition*. Oil on cardboard, $12^{1}/_{2} \times 19^{3}/_{8}''$. Musée Gustave Moreau, Paris. Ill. p. 108

*188 *Galatea*. (c. 1895). Oil on canvas, $91 \times 47^{1}/_{2}''$. Musée Gustave Moreau, Paris. Ill. p. 137

189 *The Death of Inspiration (Les lyres mortes)*. (c. 1897). Oil on canvas, $91^{1}/_{2} \times 48''$. Musée Gustave Moreau, Paris

*190 *Polyphemus*. Oil on canvas, $18^{1}/_{8} \times 15''$. Musée Gustave Moreau, Paris. Ill. p. 131

*191 *Sketch A*. Oil on wood, $8^{5}/_{8} \times 10^{5}/_{8}''$. Musée Gustave Moreau, Paris. Ill. p. 141

*192 *Sketch B*. Oil on cardboard, $15^{3}/_{4} \times 12^{1}/_{2}''$. Musée Gustave Moreau, Paris. Ill. p. 115

*193 *Sketch C*. Oil on canvas, $10^{5}/_{8} \times 8''$. Musée Gustave Moreau, Paris. Ill. p. 143

*194 *Sketch D*. Oil on cardboard, $18^{1}/_{2} \times 12^{1}/_{2}''$. Musée Gustave Moreau, Paris. Ill. p. 139

*195 *Sketch E*. Oil on wood, $12^{5}/_{8} \times 9^{7}/_{8}''$. Musée Gustave Moreau, Paris. Ill. p. 140

MOREAU: WATERCOLORS AND DRAWINGS

196 *Salome*. (c. 1875). Pencil, $23^{1}/_{2} \times 13^{5}/_{8}''$. Musée Gustave Moreau, Paris.

197 *The Apparition*. (c. 1876). Watercolor, $41^{3}/_{4} \times 28^{1}/_{4}''$. Cabinet des Dessins du Musée du Louvre, Paris

198 *The Hydra*. (c. 1876). Pencil, $7 \times 6''$. Collection Georges Wildenstein

*199 *Phaeton*. (Before 1878). Watercolor, $13^{1}/_{2} \times 10''$. Study for large drawing. Musée Gustave Moreau, Paris. Ill. p. 131

200 *Phaeton*. (c. 1878). Watercolor, $39 \times 9''$. Cabinet des Dessins du Musée du Louvre, Paris.

201 *Europa and the Bull*. Watercolor, $6 \times 5''$. Wadsworth Atheneum, Hartford, Connecticut. The Ella Gallup Sumner and Mary Catlin Sumner Collection

202 *La Toilette.* Watercolor. 13×7¹/₂″. Collection Georges Wildenstein

*203 *The Rat from the City and the Rat from the Country.* (1881). Watercolor, 11³/₈×8¹/₄″. Sketch for "The Fables of La Fontaine." Musée Gustave Moreau, Paris. Ill. p. 126

*204 Study (probably for *The Chimeras*). (Begun in 1884). Watercolor, 12⁷/₈×9¹/₂″. Musée Gustave Moreau, Paris. Ill. p. 122

*205 *Ganymede.* Watercolor, 9³/₄×13³/₄″. Musée Gustave Moreau, Paris. Ill. p. 127

206 *Hercules and the Doe.* Watercolor, 8³/₄×6″. Musée Gustave Moreau, Paris

*207 *Salome.* Watercolor, 15×9³/₄″. Musée Gustave Moreau, Paris. Ill. p. 120

208 *Woman and Panther.* Watercolor, 11³/₄×7⁷/₈″. Musée Gustave Moreau, Paris

*209 *Combat of the Centaurs.* Watercolor, 5⁷/₈×11″. Musée Gustave Moreau, Paris. Ill. p. 134

*210 *Narcissus.* Watercolor, 21⁷/₈×23⁷/₈″. Musée Gustave Moreau, Paris. Ill. p. 133

*211 *The Temptation of St. Anthony.* (c. 1890). Watercolor, 5¹/₈×9³/₈″. Musée Gustave Moreau, Paris. Ill. p. 135

*212 *The Death of Inspiration (Les lyres mortes).* (c. 1895–97). Watercolor, 15×9³/₄″. Musée Gustave Moreau, Paris. Sketch for oil of same title, No. 188. Ill. p. 130

213 *Sketch.* Watercolor, 8×12¹/₂″. Musée Gustave Moreau, Paris

BRESDIN: PRINTS

Unless otherwise indicated, the lender is The Art Institute of Chicago (The Walter S. Brewster Collection). Measurements refer to the composition.

"Boon" and "Neumann" followed by a number refer to the following catalogues:

Rodolphe Bresdin. *Etsen en Lithografieën,* Amsterdam, 1955. (Preface by I. Q. van Regteren Altena; introduction and catalogue by K. G. Boon).

J. B. Neumann (editor). *Rodolphe Bresdin* in *The Art Lover Library,* Volume I (picture catalogue), 1929.

Etchings

214 *Trees in the Wind.* (c. 1840). 5¹/₁₆×7⁵/₈″. Boon 7, Neumann 66

215 *The Mountain Lake.* (c. 1856–57). Etching published in *Revue Fantaisiste,* 1861. 4⁷/₈×4³/₈″. Boon 51, Neumann 95

216 *The Holy Family with a Pole.* 1858. 2×4³/₁₆″. Boon 55, Neumann 94

*217 *Bathers in a Mountain Landscape.* (c. 1858). 7¹/₈× 9⁷/₈″ (plate). Boon 60, Neumann 99. Ill. p. 152

218 *River Town with a Stone Bridge.* 1860. 9³/₈×6⁵/₁₆″ (plate). Boon 65, Neumann 106
a. First state
b. Second state

219 *Thatched Cottages (Entrée de village).* 1861. Etching published in *Revue Fantaisiste,* 1861. 5⁹/₁₆×3¹⁵/₁₆″. Boon 62, Neumann 29

*220 *Forest of Fontainebleau.* 8×5⁷/₈″. Boon 64, Neumann 30. Ill. p. 156

221 *Flemish Interior.* Etching published in *Revue Fantaisiste,* 1861. 6¹/₄×4¹/₄″. Boon 72, Neumann 22

222 *Death and the Young Mother.* Etching published in *Revue Fantaisiste,* 1861. 5¹/₁₆×3⁷/₁₆″. Boon 75, Neumann 25

223 *Knight and Death* (also called: *Le chateau fort*). 1866. 5⁷/₈×8³/₄″. Boon 87, Neumann 38. The Metropolitan Museum of Art. Gift of F. H. Hirschland; The J. B. Neumann Collection, 1952

*224 *Oriental Rider in a Rocky Landscape.* 1866. 11³/₄× 9″ (plate). Boon 89, Neumann 109. Ill. p. 157

225 *Departure for the Hunt.* 1869. 9¹⁵/₁₆×13¹/₂″. Boon 104

226 *The Knight.* 1871. 2¹⁵/₁₆×6¹/₈″. Neumann 105 A (first state)

227 *The Holy Family with a Grazing Donkey.* 1871. 9×7¹³/₁₆″. Boon 57, Neumann 55 B. George A. Lucas Collection, The Maryland Institute. On permanent loan to the Baltimore Museum of Art

228 *The Stream.* 1880. 6³/₄×9⁵/₈″. Boon 113, Neumann 35. The Metropolitan Museum of Art. Gift of F. H. Hirschland; The J. B. Neumann Collection, 1951

*229 *A Clearing in the Forest.* 1880. 9×6″. Boon 114, Neumann 39. Ill. p. 146

Book

230 *Revue Fantaisiste*, Paris; Second volume, May 15–
    August 1, 1861 (contains 7 etchings by Bresdin)

Lithographs

*231 *The Holy Family beside a Rushing Stream.* Dated
     1835 (1853?). $8^7/_8 \times 6^{13}/_{16}''$. Boon 43, Neumann 53.
     Ill. p. 151

*232 *The Comedy of Death.* 1854. Lithograph transferred
     from etching, $8^9/_{16} \times 5^{13}/_{16}''$. Boon 45, Neumann 44.
     Ill. p. 154

233 *Female Bather and Time.* 1857. $6^1/_4 \times 4^5/_{16}''$. Boon
    53, Neumann 119

234 *Female Bather and Death.* 1857. $6^5/_{16} \times 4^5/_{16}''$.
    Boon 54, Neumann 120

*235 *The Good Samaritan.* 1861. $22^1/_8 \times 17^3/_8''$. Boon 76,
     Neumann 49. Frontispiece

*236 *The Holy Family with the Does* (also called: *The
     Holy Family with the Ducks*). 1868. $10^3/_8 \times 7^7/_8''$.
     Boon 93, Neumann 54. Ill. p. 158

237 *Chateau in the Mountains.* 1868. $7 \times 4^3/_8''$. Boon 95,
    Neumann 59

238 Frontispiece for *Le Calvaire du Vieux Caillou.* 1868.
    $9^3/_8 \times 7^5/_8''$. Neumann 48 (first state). Collection Mr.
    and Mrs. Leonard Baskin, Northampton, Massa-
    chusetts

239 *The Enchanted Castle.* 1871. $6^3/_4 \times 9^5/_8''$. Boon 105,
    Neumann 42

240 *Fishing Boats in Port.* 1883. $19 \times 12^3/_{16}''$. Boon 120,
    Neumann 117

BRESDIN: DRAWINGS

Unless otherwise indicated, the owner is The Art Institute
of Chicago (The Walter S. Brewster Collection).

241 *Caucasian Landscape.* Signed and dated "Caillou
    185(?)." Pen and India ink, $5 \times 6^1/_2''$

242 *The Smugglers.* Signed and dated "Rodolphe Bres-
    din 1858." Pen and India ink, $5^1/_2 \times 8^3/_4''$

*243 *The Crevasse.* Signed and dated "Rodolphe Bresdin
     1860." Pen and India ink, $8^5/_{16} \times 6^1/_2''$. Ill. p. 153

*244 *Studies for The Good Samaritan.* Pen and India ink,
     $7^{11}/_{16} \times 9''$. The Municipal Museum, The Hague.
     Ill. p. 149

245 *Stream in a Gorge.* Pen and India ink, $5^3/_8 \times 8^5/_8''$

246 *Bathers in a Brook.* Pen and India ink, $4^1/_2 \times 6^{13}/_{16}''$

*247 *Bank of a Pond.* Pen and India ink, $6^7/_{16} \times 6^{11}/_{16}''$.
     Ill. p. 155

*248 *City in the Mountains.* Pen and India ink, $6^1/_2 \times
     4^7/_{16}''$. Ill. p. 155

249 *Rocky Seashore.* Pen and India ink, $3^1/_8 \times 4^5/_{16}''$.

250 *Landscape with an Old Church.* Pen and India ink,
    $4^3/_8 \times 4^3/_8''$

251 *Old Houses and Fishing Boats.* Pen and India ink,
    $6^{11}/_{16} \times 4^5/_8''$

252 *Arab Horsemen.* Pen and India ink, $5 \times 4^1/_2''$

253 *An Indian in Costume.* Signed and dated "Bresdin
    Rodolphe 1878." Pen and India ink, $6^5/_8 \times 5^3/_8''$

254 *Nightmare.* Pen and India ink, $7^1/_8 \times 4^3/_4''$. The Met-
    ropolitan Museum of Art, New York. Gift of F. H.
    Hirschland; The J. B. Neumann Collection, 1952

255 *River.* Pen and India ink, $7^5/_8 \times 6^3/_4''$. The Metro-
    politan Museum of Art, New York. Gift of F. H.
    Hirschland; The J. B. Neumann Collection, 1951

256 *Beached Galleons.* Pen and India ink, $6^7/_8 \times 4^3/_4''$.
    The Metropolitan Museum of Art, New York. Gift
    of F. H. Hirschland; The J. B. Neumann Collection,
    1951

*257 *Aqueduct and Waterfalls.* Pen and India ink, $4^5/_8 \times
     4^3/_4''$. Collection Mr. and Mrs. Leonard Baskin,
     Northampton, Massachusetts. Ill. p. 159

INDEX

1217